PREFACE

This booklet has been written to give a br__ _____, __ ___ most important aspects of the culture of the Indians of Virginia in the seventeenth century. Due to the lack of space, certain less important facets of their culture have been omitted.

This simplified picture of the Virginia Indians pertains largely to the historic Powhatan Indians or the confederated Algonquian tribes in the state. This is necessary for the simple reason that practically all the source materials we have on the Virginia Indians of the seventeenth century relate to the Powhatan Confederacy. For example, we have no description of a Siouan village in the Virginia Piedmont. The few records we have for the Piedmont, for the mountains and valleys beyond, are often too vague to be reliable. Nor can we assume that John Lawson's invaluable account of the Siouan Indians of the Carolinas of the early eighteenth century will describe the Siouans of Virginia. There was a marked difference in the languages spoken by these two groups, and it is believed that there were distinct cultural differences.

By the middle of the seventeenth century most of the Indian settlements in the upper valleys of the James and Rappahannock rivers had been abandoned. Very few Indians were in the Piedmont in 1675. Many had succumbed to the white man's diseases, and the remainder had migrated or had been exterminated by hostile Indian nations from the north.

In order to provide greater appreciation and understanding of the culture of our historic Indians, I have appended a concise review of the prehistory of Virginia. This is based on the archaeological work done in the state—which regrettably has been neglected—and that done in adjacent states having comparable Indian cultures. I have also added a bibliography of the most important source materials and other works consulted in the preparation of this booklet.

B. C. M.

The Geographic Position, Names, and Population of the Indian Tribes in Virginia in 1607

At the beginning of the seventeenth century, the area now included in Virginia was inhabited by many tribes belonging to three linguistic stocks, the Algonquian, the Iroquoian, and the Siouan.

The Algonquian Tribes

The Algonquian tribes occupied the land in Virginia east of a line running from Washington, D. C., through Fredericksburg, Richmond, Petersburg, and then turning southeast along the Blackwater River and extending into coastal North Carolina as far as the Neuse River. They also inhabited the two counties Accomack and Northampton in the present Eastern Shore, Virginia. The Algonquians pushed down into Virginia from the north centuries before the coming of the English. It remains for archaeology to determine approximately when this movement took place. Shortly before the English colony was established at Jamestown in 1607, chief Powhatan had brought under his control by conquest most of the Algonquian tribes in the tidewater country. This recently formed confederacy was held together by his despotic power. He had inherited only the territories of Powhatan, Arrohattoc, Appomattoc, Pamunkey, Youghtanund, and Mattapanient (Mattaponi), all of which were within fifty miles of the present Richmond.

Smith enumerates twenty-eight tribes in the confederacy, but shows on his map thirty-six "king's houses" or tribal capitals. A manuscript of 1622 gives "32 Kingdomes." Therefore, it can be said that Powhatan had more than thirty provinces, or kingdoms or tribes under his rule. Within these provinces, Smith's map shows a total of 161 villages, large and small.

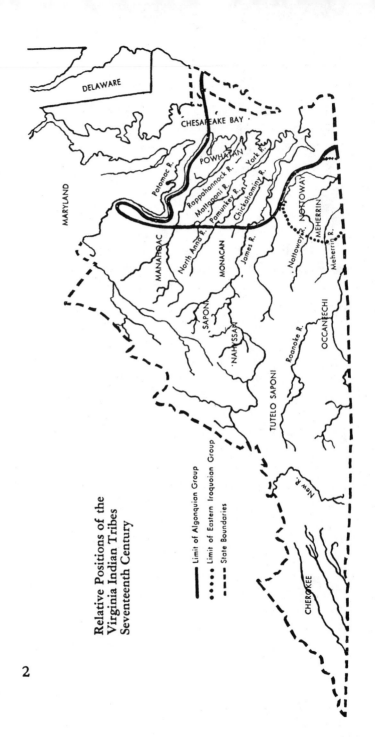

Relative Positions of the
Virginia Indian Tribes
Seventeenth Century

—— Limit of Algonquian Group
•••••• Limit of Eastern Iroquoian Group
– – – State Boundaries

DELAWARE

CHESAPEAKE BAY

MARYLAND

POWHATAN

Potomac R.

Rappahannock R.

Mattaponi R.

Pamunkey R.

York R.

Chickahominy R.

North Anna R.

MANAHOAC

MONACAN

James R.

SAPON

NAHYSSAN

NOTTOWAY

Nottoway R.

MEHERRIN

Meherrin R.

OCCANEECHI

Roanoke R.

TUTELO SAPONI

New R.

CHEROKEE

2

THE CHIEF ALGONQUIAN TRIBES UNDER POWHATAN'S RULE OR INFLUENCE

Accohannoc. The territory of this tribe was in the area of the present boundary of Northampton and Accomack counties. Their principal village was on the present Occohannock Creek. Population about 150.

Accomac. This important tribe lived in the area around the present Cape Charles city. Their principal village was located some distance inland from the bay on Cherrystone Creek. Population about 300. In 1608 Kictopeake was the chief of this tribe. His brother Debedeavon "the laughing king of the Accomacks," whose village was situated on Nandua Creek, was the overlord or great werowance of all the small communities or villages on the Eastern Shore. All the Indians of the Eastern Shore were commonly referred to by the colonists as Accomacks.

Appomattoc. Appamattucks, chief village of King Coquonasum was located until 1623 on Swift Creek, a tributary of the Appomattox River, about a mile above its mouth. Apamatuks (Smith) or Mattica (Tindall) was the chief village of Queen Oppussoquionuske, sister of King Coquonasum. It was located on Bermuda Hundred point until it was destroyed about Christmas, 1611, by Sir Thomas Dale.

Appomattocks Indian Towne apparently became the chief village after the destruction in 1623 of King Coquonasum's village by Capt. Nathaniel West. It was located on Old Indian Towne Creek, the present Rohoic Run, and remained there until 1691. It was within a short distance of the site of Fort Henry, 1646-1676. Population about 250.

Arrohattoc. The chief town was located about 12 miles below Richmond on the north bank of the James River, just above Dutch Gap and the Dutch Gap Canal in Henrico County. Population about 120.

Chesapeake. This tribe occupied land between the Elizabeth

River and the ocean. Their principal town was near the mouth of the Lynnhaven River in Princess Anne County. Population about 375.

Chickahominy. This large and important tribe lived along the Chickahominy River in James City, Charles City and New Kent counties. Their territory very likely extended from the region of Parsons Island and Wright Island up the Chickahominy River to the western region of Charles City and New Kent counties. Smith indicated that the concentration of these people was very heavy in the area near the present Lanexa. Population about 940.

Chiskiack (Kiskiack). This was the only tribe which was living in 1608 along the York River from the fork of the river to its mouth. Their territory, primarily in York County along the river, perhaps extended inland to the headwaters of the creeks flowing into the river. Artifacts of late Indian occupancy have been found along Queens Creek, Kings Creek, Felgates Creek, Indian Field Creek and in the Naval Mine Depot area. Historical students locate the tribe's town in the vicinity of Indian Field Creek. It could have been on the bluff overlooking Indian Field Creek. A row of houses occupied by naval officers has perhaps disturbed part of the archaeological evidence, but a sufficient amount remains on the wooded end of the bluff to suggest a village site in the immediate vicinity. Population about 190.

Cuttatawomen. There were two chief towns by this name. One stood at the junction of the Corotoman River and the Rappahannock River, in Lancaster County. Population about 115. The other chief town was on the Rappahannock River at the mouth of Lamb Creek, in King George County. Population about 75.

Kecoughtan. The Kecoughtan Indians lived on both sides of Hampton River in Elizabeth City County. Smith's and Tindall's maps place the Indian town on the east side or Phoebus side of Hampton River. Population about 75.

Mattaponi. A tribe that lived along the Mattaponi River. Their

4

main territory was probably in King William County. Population about 115.

Moraughtacund. This tribe lived on the north bank of the Rappahannock River in Richmond and Lancaster counties. Their chief village was at the junction of the Morattico River and the Rappahannock River. Population about 300.

Nansemond. A rather large tribe with extensive territory in Isle of Wight, Nansemond, and Norfolk counties. They evidently ranged the Dismal Swamp east and southeast of Suffolk. Their principal village was at Reid's Ferry near the present Chuckatuck. Population about 750.

Nantaughtacund. A tribe living on the south bank of the Rappahannock River, in Essex and Caroline counties. The chief town was on the south shore of a large bay known today as Port Tabago or Port Tobacco Bay. Population about 575.

Onawmanient. This tribe lived in Westmoreland County, about Nominy Bay. Population about 375.

Pamunkey. This large tribe lived on the neck of land in King William County formed by the confluence of the Pamunkey and the Mattaponi rivers. One of the principal villages was Cinquoateck located where the present West Point now stands. Another important village was Menapucunt (Menapacant) located in the big bend in the Pamunkey River just above West Point. Population about 1,100.

Paspahegh. The territory of this tribe extended east as well as west of the Chickahominy where it flows into the James. Their principal town was at Sandy Point on the James River in Charles City County. Population about 160.

Piankatank. A tribe that lived on the north side of the Piankatank River in Middlesex County. Their principal village was at Turk's Ferry. Population about 200.

Pissaseck. This tribe lived on the north bank of the Rappahannock in King George and Westmoreland and Richmond counties. Its "Kings howse" or chief village stood just above the present Leedstown. No population figures are available but the large number of surface artifacts recovered during recent years indicate that it was a village of great extent.

Patawomeke (Potomac). A large tribe from which it is believed the name of the Potomac River was derived. Their principal village site was in Stafford County at the mouth of the Potomac Creek. (It was here that Captain Argall kidnapped Pocahontas in April 1613.) Population about 750.

Powhatan. A small tribe which lived on the north bank of the James River, in Henrico County, below the falls at the present Richmond. The village is described as being one mile below the falls, opposite three fertile islands. The chief of the village was Parahunt, called by the English Tanxpowatan or Little Powhatan, one of the sons of the Great Powhatan or Wahunsonacock who was living at Werowocomoco when the English settled at Jamestown in 1607. Population of Powhatan about 150.

Quiyoughcohanock (Tapahanock). This tribe lived about the present Grays Creek and Chippoak Creek on the south side of the James River in Surry County. Its chief town was on the upper part of Chippoak Creek. Population about 100.

Rappahannock (frequently called Toppahanock). An important tribe that lived on the north bank of the Rappahannock River in Richmond County. Their territory extended along the north side of the river from a short distance below Totuskey Creek to a point well above Rappahannock Creek (Cat Point Creek today). Their principal village was on the present Cat Point Creek. Surface artifacts indicate that they had a rather large village at the mouth of Little Carter Creek. Population about 380.

Secacawoni (Cekacawon). This tribe lived in Northumberland County, along the Coan River and near its entrance into the Potomac River. Population about 110.

6

Tauxenent. A tribe which lived along the Potomac River in Fairfax County. Their principal village was at, or near Mount Vernon. Population about 150.

Warrasqueoc. This tribe lived in the northern part of Isle of Wight County. Their principal village was at the mouth of the present Pagan Creek on the eastern edge of Burwell's Bay, near the present Smithfield. Population about 150.

Weanoc. An important tribe that held land in 1607 on both banks of the James River extending from Appomattox River down as far as Chippoak Creek, or most of the land in northern Prince George County and in southern Charles City County. Later in the century the records indicate that they occupied some land in Surry County. Smith places their king's house on the north bank of the James almost opposite the mouth of the Appomattox River, or certainly some distance west of the present Weyanoke. Tindall's map shows "Wynagh" on the south bank of the James which may have led one student (Tyler) to place the principal village near the head of Powell's Creek in Prince George County. In the early days of the colony the land on the north side of the James was referred to as Little (Tanx) Weyanoke, and that on the south side as Greater Weyanoke. Population about 380.

Werowocomoco. Those who maintain that Powhatan's principal residence was located in 1608 to 1609 at Poetan Bay on the north bank of the York River seem to have the better of the argument. This bay is about 11 miles below West Point. It was apparently called Poetan by Tindall on his map of 1608 because Powhatan lived there. Some investigators have argued in favor of a site near Rosewell. Smith's description of the site could apply to Poetan Bay as well as to the area around the mouth of Cedar Bush Creek at Blundering Point. The latter site has produced many Indian artifacts of the late Woodland type. The population at Werowocomoco was about 150. In January 1609,

Powhatan changed his residence to Orapaks in the wilderness between the upper Chickahominy and Pamunkey rivers.

Wicocomoco (Wighcocomoco). This tribe lived in Northumberland County on the south side of the Potomac River, near its entrance into the Chesapeake Bay. Their principal village was on Wicocomico River. Population about 490.

Youghtanund. This tribe lived along the upper part of the Pamunkey River. They may have lived on both sides of the river, but probably for the most part on the south side in Hanover County. Population about 230.

THE IROQUOIAN TRIBES

Three Iroquoian tribes lived in Virginia; the Cherokee, the Nottoway or Mangoac, and the Meherrin.

Cherokee. The Cherokee had control of the narrow southwestern part of Virginia beyond the Blue Ridge. They wandered in and out frequently and were never perhaps very numerous because their homeland was western North Carolina and eastern Tennessee.

Nottoway. The Nottoway or Mangoac were related to the Tuscarora of North Carolina, and lived in the southeastern part of Virginia along the Nottoway River. Their territory extended into North Carolina along the Chowan River as far as Albemarle Sound. In the early years of the 17th century, they numbered about 1,500.

Meherrin. The Meherrin lived along the river of the same name in southeastern Virginia and northeastern North Carolina. This tribe was closely allied with the Nottoway. Later in the 17th century they received an influx of Conestoga Indians. In the early part of the 17th century they probably had a population of 700.

THE SIOUAN TRIBES

Manahoac. Manahoac Indians of Siouan stocks inhabited most of the remaining territory in Virginia. The Manahoac inhabited

8

northern Virginia from the mountains to the fall line, and from the Potomac to the North Anna River. Their main area of concentration was about the upper waters of the Rappahannock River. Smith gives us the name of seven Siouan tribes in this area which were "contributers" to the Manahoac. They were as follows: Hassinnungas, Outponcas, Shackaconias, Stegarakes, Tauxsnitanias, Tegoneaes, and Whonkentyaes (Smith's spelling). In 1600 they had a population of perhaps 1,500.

Monacan. Smith tells us that the Monacan and the Manahoac and their "contributers" were all confederates. Monacan refers to a tribe and a confederacy which held the land along the James River from the vicinity of the falls west to the Blue Ridge. The names of five villages connected with this group are given on Smith's map. They are: Mowhemcho, Massinacack, Rassawek, Monasukapanough, and Monahassanugh. It is probable that the last two towns mentioned did not form a part of the confederacy, and they will therefore be treated here separately as Saponi and as Tutelo. Captain Newport visited two of the towns, Mowhemcho and Massinacack, in 1608. According to Bushnell, Mowhemcho stood on the south bank of the James in the extreme eastern part of Powhatan County, between Bernards Creek and Jones Creek. Bushnell places Massinacack on the south bank of the James at the mouth of the present Mohawk Creek, about one and one-half miles south of the town of Goochland, on the opposite side of the James River. Smith says that the chief town of the Monacans was at Rassawek. Rassawek was probably located, as suggested by Smith's map, at the confluence of the James and the Rivanna rivers. Population about 1,500.

Saponi. This name was possibly a contraction of Monasukapanough, the name of a tribe located on Smith's map in the Monacan country. Bushnell places their earliest known village site on the banks of the Rivanna in Albemarle County, directly north of the University of Virginia, about one-half mile up the river from the bridge of the Southern Railway. Thomas Jefferson, many years later, opened the burial mound which stood on the Indian town site. Population about 1,200.

Tutelo. This name was used by the Iroquois to refer to the Siouan tribes of the south generally. It is used here to refer to the Monahassanugh of Smith or Tutelo or Nahyssan of later narratives. Bushnell believed that their oldest known village was on the left bank of the James River about one and one-half miles up the stream from Wingina in Nelson County. Population about 1,000.

Mohetan. The Mohetan or Moketan, about whom we have only one authority, lived in the mountains about the upper waters of the New River. Population unknown.

Occaneechi. This small but important tribe lived on an island in Roanoke River near the present Clarksville, in Mecklenburg County. Population 1,200.

Total Population. Mooney has estimated that the population of the Powhatan confederacy was 9,000 in 1607. It is believed that the agricultural and fishing habits of the tidewater Indians were conducive to a larger population than in any other section of the state where the people were mostly nomadic. At any rate, conservative estimates have given the Indians living in the remaining four-fifths of the area of Virginia a population equal to that of the tidewater Indians. This would give an approximate population figure of 18,000 for the entire state.

SOCIAL ORGANIZATION

Powhatan inherited six tribes, Arrohattoc, Appomattoc, Mattaponi, Pamunkey, Powhatan, and Youghtanund, all within fifty miles of the present Richmond. A few years before the arrival of the English, he had built a large confederacy. To his small inheritance he had added by force and treachery, twenty-five or more tribes and nearly all the territory comprising the Virginia Tidewater.

10

Tribes living some distance away along the Rappahannock, the Potomac, and the Eastern Shore area formed parts of the confederacy but their ties were weaker than those of tribes closer to Powhatan's inherited tribes. It is true that the Chickahominy were close to the center of the confederacy, but they were numerous and successfully resisted the great werowance's direct control over them.

Each of the thirty-odd chief towns under Powhatan had apportioned to it a certain amount of land over which ruled a local chief or werowance. The members of each tribe knew the land ascribed to them and upon which they could hunt and fish. Every werowance was subject to Powhatan, or to a greater werowance who was subject in turn to Powhatan. A local werowance might have one or several towns under his rule. Government was arbitrary and tyrannical, and the power of the local werowances apparently extended to life and death over their subjects.

Powhatan was a crafty, ambitious and capable man. He was well equipped physically. Smith describes him as "a tall well proportioned man, with a sower looke, his head somewhat gray, his beard so thinne, that it seemeth none at all, his age (as of 1608) neare sixtie, of a very able and hardy body to endure any labour." The people looked upon him as a king and as a half god. He had the power of life and death over his subjects, and instilled great fear in them. Severe beatings were given for ordinary corrections, and horrible death by fire, by piecemeal amputation, or by clubbing constituted the punishment for more serious offenses.

Although Powhatan held the reins of government in his hands, the assistance he received from members of his family made his task easier. For example, his three brothers, Opitchapan, Opechancanough, and Kecatough ruled over the heavily populated area of the present Pamunkey River; his son Parahunt was seated at the present Richmond; and another son, Pochins was chief of the Kecoughtan.

In 1607, Powhatan (Wahunsonacock was his proper name) had his favorite residence at Werowocomoco on the north side of the York. The English found him there in 1608, but in January 1609, he moved to Orapaks in the extreme western part of New Kent County, in order to be further removed from the English settlement at Jamestown. He always kept around him a guard of forty or fifty of the tallest men of his country. His councilors consisted of priests, conjurers, werowances (men and women), ancient friends and allies, brought together in a body at his residence to advise him on important matters. Questions such as preparations for war, a victory, or any occasion for great rejoicing necessitated a council meeting.

The influence of the priests was important and sometimes strong enough to determine the course of action of the great werowance. Smith tells us that when the werowances intended any wars, they usually had the advice of their priests, and that their resolutions were chiefly determined by the priests.

An important element in the governmental system of the Powhatan confederacy was the paying of tribute. This tribute not only kept the wealth in Powhatan's hands, but also served as a continuous acknowledgment of the submission of the werowances to Powhatan, and of their readiness to follow him to his wars. The great werowance made personal visits in his inherited territory to collect the tribute, and sent for it in the more distant parts of his kingdom. Strachey tells us that every werowance paid him "eight parts of ten tribute of all the comodities which their country yeldeth." Tribute consisted of corn, beans, skins, copper, beads, pearls, turkeys, deer and other wild animals.

Another feature of their organization which is worthy of observation was the rule relative to the succession to a werowance or to the great werowance. Lineal issue was excluded from succeeding immediately to the crown, or in other words, they reckoned descent in the female line. Powhatan's kingdom was not to pass in a direct line to his children but to his brothers and after their deaths to his sisters, first to the eldest, then to the rest, and after them to the male or female heirs of the eldest sister, "and never to the heirs of the males."

The Siouan tribes in Virginia were usually smaller and more widely scattered than the Algonquian. Swanton says that the Siouan chiefs were in some cases just as absolute as Powhatan. In most cases questions were argued and settled in councils consisting of the head chief, his captains and advisers. Among the Siouans the succession fell not to the chief's son, but to his sister's son. In the manner of the Powhatan, the Siouan people looked upon their chiefs with fear and respect.

Inheritance does not seem to have played an important part among the Cherokee. Most of the chiefs were self-made men. There was apparently no developed aristocracy. However, we know very little of the seventeenth century Cherokee tribes in Virginia.

VILLAGES

Archaeological evidence and the early narratives prove that the Indians in Virginia of the historic period built their villages near rivers, streams, or near large springs. When they were built near a river, they were usually on a rise that protected them from floods and, at the same time, commanded a good view of the river. The villages were usually small, consisting of from two to fifty or occasionally one hundred houses. The arrangement of the houses did not follow any regular pattern. The buildings of a large village were often scattered over a hundred or more acres. Isolated houses often stood some distance from the main village.

Some villages were encircled by a fence or fortification of strong poles ten or twelve feet high set close together in the ground, and providing only one narrow entrance. In the large villages, the palisade enclosed only the most important houses, and there was necessarily a more orderly arrangement of the

13

houses. They were usually built close to the enclosure with an open space in the center.

There is no description preserved of a Siouan or Iroquoian village in Virginia of the seventeenth century, and it is not known to what extent they palisaded their town. Tribes of both groups are known to have protected their villages with palisades in the early eighteenth century, which leads one to believe that their villages were similarly protected in Virginia in the seventeenth century.

HOUSES

The houses built by the Powhatan Indians were typical of the Algonquian wigwams. The framework consisted of small green poles whose thickest ends were set in the ground, from two to three feet apart, in a circular or oblong rectangular shape. The smaller houses tended to be round and the larger more oblong. The tops of the opposite poles were bent over and tied firmly together with strips of bark or fibrous roots. The framework of the ends of the rectangular type house was made of upright poles. Smaller horizontal poles or braces were added to the entire structure.

The coverings of this arched framework consisted of large pieces of bark, or of mats made of rushes. The leaves of the flag or cat-o'-nine-tails were probably strung together on cords of fibrous bark, Indian hemp, or silk grass for making mats. The mats were three or four feet wide by eight or ten feet long, and bound at each end to a small pole, one or two inches in diameter, which was provided with tying cords. Cords were also attached along the edges of the mats.

Bark was preferred for the coverings of the more important and permanent houses. Mats were sometimes used for roofs and bark for the walls. There were no windows, but in summer the bark was removed or the mats rolled up around the lower part of the wigwams to make them more open and airy.

It should be noted that Robert Beverley, writing in 1705, states

14

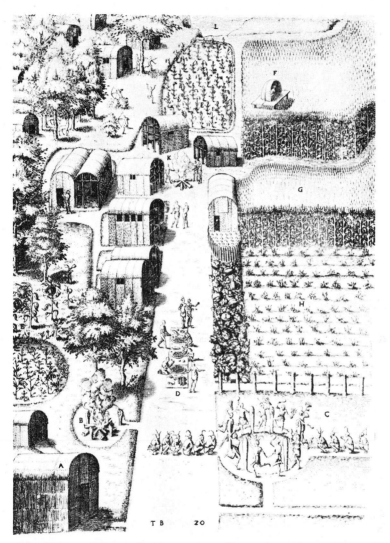

"The Town of Secota," Algonquian village situated on the north bank of Pamlico River in the present Beaufort County, N. C.
(A) tomb of their kings, (B) plot where they assemble to pray, (C) where they celebrate feasts, (D) where they make merry after feast, (E) tobacco garden, (F) ripe corn and hut for watchman, (G) green corn, (H) corn recently sprouted, (I) pumpkin garden, (K) fire built at feast time, (L) river. Photographed from the printed version in Thomas Hariot, *A Brief and True Report* . . . (French edition, Frankfort, 1590), plate **XX**.

"The towne of Pomeiock and true forme of their howses."

The Algonquian Indian village of Pomeiock was situated near the mouth of Gibbs Creek, now in Hyde County, North Carolina. White describes the houses as "couered and enclosed some with matts, and some with the barcks of trees. All compassed about with small poles stuck thick together in stedd of a wall."

The mat-covered sleeping benches may clearly be seen inside the walls of three of the houses in the background.

From color reproduction by Charles Praetorius of an original water color drawing by John White, made in 1585, while a member of the expedition financed by Sir Walter Raleigh which founded the ill-fated English colony on Roanoke Island, Virginia (now N.C.). Photograph by The Smithsonian Institution

"One of the wyues of the Wyngyno" (a young gentlewoman daughter of Secota) By John White. Photograph by The Smithsonian Institution.

"A Weroan or great lord of Virginia" ("The manner of their attire and painting themselves") By John White. Photograph by The Smithsonian Institution.

that the houses did have windows. "Their windows are little holes left open for the passage of the Light, which in bad weather they stop with shutters of the same bark, opening the leeward windows for air and light." Since Strachey specifically says, "Wyndowes they have none," and the other early writers make no mention of them, it is apparent that they were an innovation introduced after white contact.

The larger rectangular houses had a door at each end, hung with mats which could be rolled up. A small hole was left in the top-center to allow the smoke to escape from the fire which was always built in the middle of the wigwam. All the early narratives attest that the wigwams were as warm as stoves but very smoky.

Small houses of the circular type were constructed very quickly. When the men were on their hunting trips, the women were sent ahead with mats to the appointed place to build houses for the hunters to lie in at night.

Hariot provides us with the following measurements of the ordinary oblong dwelling: "The length of them is commonly double to the breadth, in some places they are but 12 and 16 yardes long, and in other some wee have seene of foure and twentie." The kings' houses were broader and longer than the others and apparently had several partitions or inner chambers. Powhatan had a house in each of his inherited provinces. These were of the oblong type, and according to Smith, "Built after their manner like arbours, some 30, some 40 yards long, and at every house provision for his entertainement according to the time."

Strachey tells us that by their houses they sometimes built a scaffold of small reeds or osiers which was covered with mats, forming a shelter for recreation or pleasure, and where, on a loft of hurdles, "They laye forth their corne and fish to dry."

The ordinary house had only one room. The beds consisted of hurdles or platforms placed along the wall about one foot above the ground on forked posts. Smith's description is as follows: "They lie on little hurdles of reeds, covered with a mat, borne from the ground a foote and more by a hurdle of wood. On these round about the house they lie heads and points one by the other against the fire, some covered with mats, some with skins, and some starke naked lie on the ground, from 6 to 20 in a house."

The houses of the Virginia Siouan were probably very similar to the Algonquian wigwam. Lawson's description of the North Carolina Siouan houses suggests this similarity.

The Iroquoian houses in Virginia in the seventeenth century were perhaps similar to those of the Cherokee farther south. The walls consisted of thick posts fixed in the ground at regular intervals. Between each of these posts was placed a smaller post, and the whole matted with twigs and covered over with clay or moss. Narrow boards served as rafters which were covered with large pieces of bark. A small hole in the top provided some escape for the smoke. The Meherrin Indians probably used this type of construction. There is some evidence that the Nottoway used the wigwam type of house.

FOODS

The houses of an Algonquian village were usually a short distance apart, and occasionally they were separated by small groves of trees. But whether there were few houses or many, they were in the midst of fields or cultivated gardens. Each house had a garden one hundred or two hundred feet square, and which, Strachey tells us, was kept "As neat and cleane as we doe our gardein bedds." The gardens of a small town might cover twenty acres, of a large town as much as two hundred acres.

It required much labor on the part of the Indian men to prepare new ground. The trees were killed by bruising the bark near the roots and by burning around the base to kill the roots. The following year the Indians would dig up the ground around the roots and plant their corn there.

16

In preparing a field previously cleared and cultivated, the men first loosened the soil with wooden instruments shaped very much like a hoe with a long handle. The top soil was loosened to a depth of only a few inches. Then the women took over the task. The weeds and cornstalks were piled and burned. Hariot tells us that they burned the trash only to get rid of it. They did not spread the ashes and did not seem to know anything about improving the soil. However, fertile soil usually determined their village sites.

The women worked while sitting with a planting instrument, usually a stick, about a foot long and four or five inches wide. They made rows of holes in the ground, and the rows as well as the holes were about three feet apart (Strachey says three feet and Smith says four), so that there was a space of approximately three feet between every hole in the plot. Four grains of corn and two seeds of beans were placed in each hole, and they were carefully separated and covered. In the three foot square space between the holes were often planted squash, pumpkin, sunflower, and other seeds. Sometimes a vegetable was grown in a plot by itself, but usually the method of growing them together as described above was used.

When the corn was about half grown they hilled it as we do today. The women and children were responsible for the weeding and working of the corn and other plants. Small covered platforms were often placed in the fields to provide a place for some one to guard the field from birds or animals, especially during the early season.

Planting began in April and continued until the middle of June, but the major planting was done in May. In August they harvested the April planting, in September they harvested that of May, and in October that of June. Smith tells us that every stalk "commonly beareth two ears, some 3, seldome 4, many but one, and some none. Every eare hath between 200 and 500 graines."

Beverley speaks of four varieties of corn, two early and two late. There were, however, three principal varieties: the small corn of the nature of popcorn, which grew only three or four feet high and was the earliest kind; the flint or hominy corn which had fairly large and smooth kernels of various colors— yellow, red, blue, and white; and the "she corn," better known as dent or flour corn. The popcorn variety matured rapidly and two crops could be raised in one season.

The Indians preferred the green corn to the ripened, and gathered much of it green. This also made it possible for them to use the sweet juice in the green stalks. Spelman notes that the corn was gathered in hand-baskets, which when full were emptied into larger baskets. The corn was then spread out on mats during the day to dry. At night, it was placed in a large pile and covered with mats to protect it from the dew. When it was thoroughly dry, it was placed in the houses in piles, shelled and put in "A great baskett which taketh up the best part of sum of their houses, and all this is cheefly the weomens worke."

A special day was appointed for planting Powhatan's corn. A large number of people came to do this work for the great werowance. It was his custom to favor them with beads thrown in their midst for which they would scramble. Sometimes he presented beads personally to a few chosen ones. When his corn was ripe, the people came again, gathered, shelled, and placed it in special storage houses.

In their gardens the Powhatan Indians also raised peas (Smith says the native peas were the same as those in Italy called Fagioli), pumpkins (Smith and Strachey distinguish two varieties of a pumpkin or squash, i.e., a pumpkin ["pumpeon"], and a macock which probably refers to a squash or cymling). Beans are also mentioned (identical Smith says to what "The Turkes call *Garnanses*"), sunflowers (mentioned by Beverley, apparently omitted by Smith and Strachey), gourds, maracocks (passion flower), and tobacco.

18

The sunflower (*Helianthus annuus*) was grown for its seeds which were used in making a kind of bread and broth. Tobacco, usually cultivated in a bed by itself, was used for ceremonial purposes.

It appears that the Algonquian Indians of Virginia depended more on agriculture than the Indians of other parts of the state, but they did not harvest enough to last very long. Smith says that for three parts of the year they had to live on what the country naturally afforded them.

It is believed that the Siouan tribes in Virginia raised corn, beans, and pumpkins as did all the larger tribes of the southeast. The finding of stone hoes in numerous parts of the Piedmont, and in the Valley of Virginia is proof of a certain amount of cultivation.

In 1670, the German traveler John Lederer found that the Occaneechi, a Siouan group living on an island in the Roanoke River at the present Clarksville, Virginia, had immense crops of corn, and always had on hand a year's supply of provisions as a reserve in case of attack.

We have no specific account of the cultivation of plants among the Cherokee (Iroquoian tribe of the southwestern part of Virginia) in the seventeenth century, but later records indicate that agriculture had been a part of their culture for a long time.

Natural Food Supplies

The Virginia Indians had a large supply of natural foods. Among the fruits mentioned are: huckleberries, strawberries, mulberries, raspberries, gooseberries, cherries, persimmons, wild plums, and peaches which were introduced from Europe later on in the seventeenth century.

Native wild rye and wild rice were used. Beverley speaks of sugar from the sugar maple, and it is undoubtedly true that trees were tapped by Indians during the seventeenth century in the western part of Virginia.

19

Among other foods referred to by early Virginia writers are: chestnuts, walnuts, hickory nuts, chinquapins, and acorns. Acorns had to be prepared by drying over a fire and then by boiling.

A number of wild roots were used, but it has been difficult to identify them from the description left by the early writers.

Ground nuts *(Apios tuberosa)* and tuckahoe were two of the most important roots. The term tuckahoe apparently applied to roots of various species, and especially to the Virginia wakerobin *(Peltandra virginica)*.

ANIMAL AND FISH FOOD

Deer and bear were the two most important large animals which provided the Virginia Indians with staple animal foods. The squirrel, rabbit, beaver and otter are often mentioned by early writers. Archaeological work in many parts of the state shows that the Indians depended more on the deer and squirrel than on any other animals. The wild turkey was the most important game bird. Partridges, ducks, geese, and passenger pigeons were undoubtedly eaten wherever they could be found. Bird eggs, locusts and beetles are mentioned as Powhatan articles of consumption.

Fish provided an important source of food throughout the state. Sturgeon and herring are mentioned more frequently. Archaeological evidence as well as the early narratives prove that oysters, mussels, clams, and turtles were an important part of the diet of the eastern Indians. To the above list could be added the common crab. Strachey says that the Indians rarely ate the king crab.

HUNTING AND FISHING METHODS

Many necessities of life for the Indians were obtained by hunting and fishing. Consequently, they developed to a high degree all the skills required therein. They had wonderful powers of endurance, patience, a keen sense of direction, marvelous ability to track, and expertness as bowmen.

It was absolutely essential for the Virginia Indians to be competent deer hunters, because the deer was the principal source of animal food and of raw material for clothing. Deer were found in all parts of the state, but we are told that they were more numerous in the seventeenth century toward the heads of the rivers. At certain seasons two or three hundred Powhatan Indians would gather for a great hunt and go inland for a two or three days' journey. On such occasions they would build many small fires in a large circle and place a number of men between the fires. Other Indians then proceeded to run down and kill all the deer, elk, or bear within the circle. They frequently used a complete circle of fire five or six miles in circumference and gradually directed the burning toward the center until they were close enough to shoot the entrapped game.

Another method they used was to drive the deer to some narrow point of land and force them into the river, where Indians in boats could kill them.

If a Powhatan Indian wanted to hunt alone, he had an ingenious method of stalking. He disguised himself by covering his body with the entire hide of a deer. By skillfully manipulating the stuffed head, he could easily fool the deer and get close enough for an effective shot with his bow and arrow.

In the hunting of bear, the Indians often chased them until they climbed a tree. In most cases it was then rather easy to shoot them down.

Beaver, otter, and other small animals were most frequently taken with snares.

The Indians were very proficient fishermen, and used several methods of taking fish. They had two kinds of weirs. One was made of sticks or reeds woven together to form a hedge. This hedge or frame was made fast by stakes and extended from the high water mark out into the stream to a depth of eight or ten feet. Pockets or enclosures were placed at intervals for the fish to enter, but so contrived that they could not get out. When the water was low the fish were taken in dip-nets made of silk grass.

At the falls of the rivers where the water was shallow and the current strong, the Indians had another kind of weir which consisted of dams of stones extending quite a distance across the streams, leaving spaces or tunnels at intervals. At these intervals were set large cone-shaped baskets of reeds about ten feet long by three feet wide at the broadest end. The swift current carried the fish into the baskets and wedged them so tightly together that they could not escape. Remains of rock weirs have been reported by David I. Bushnell, Jr., at the falls of the James and Rappahannock rivers.

Fire was also used in fishing. The Indians would make a fire at night on a raised hearth in their dugout canoe. One Indian kept the fire burning brightly to dazzle the eyes of the fish so that they could easily be taken with spears by the other men in each end of the boat.

The Tidewater Indians often shot fish with long arrows attached to lines. The Accomac Indians of the Eastern Shore apparently used the true fish spear.

Fishhooks are described by Smith and Strachey. The truth of their statements has been borne out by archaeological evidence from various parts of the state, in the form of bone fishhooks and a few of stone.

PREPARATION OF FOODS

The Indians preferred to gather their corn while it was still green and milky. It was boiled in their earthen pots, or roasted in the ear before the fire. The late unripened corn was parched in hot ashes and preserved for winter use. It was then often boiled with beans.

According to Beverley, hominy was made of "corn soaked, broken in a mortar, husked and then boiled in water over a

22

gentle fire, for ten or twelve hours." Both fish and flesh were often boiled with hominy.

Meal was prepared by pounding the corn in a mortar and separating it from the hulls by sifting through a basket sieve. Mixed with water, it was made into flat cakes which were then steeped in hot water and left to dry with their own heat. These cakes were frequently boiled in water to make a broth.

Wild rice and sunflower seeds, chestnuts, walnuts, and hickory nuts were pounded into meal and mixed with water to make cakes which were baked in hot ashes, or boiled.

Mettoume seeds, probably wild rice, were used for bread and buttered with deer suet. Roots of various species, which "groweth like a flagge in marshes," called tuckahoe in Virginia, were pounded into flour and used as bread.

Meats were boiled, broiled, or roasted. Fish and flesh were broiled on spits and hurdles over the fire. If they were dried thoroughly over a slow fire they could be kept for a month or more. Oysters were smoke-cured and packed in baskets for future use. Mussels and oysters were often boiled together and the resultant broth was thickened with corn meal. Bear fat provided the most important gravy.

Berries and several kinds of fruits, including peaches introduced by the whites later in the century, were dried upon mats and stored away for the winter months.

Tobacco

Tobacco was used by the Indians everywhere in Virginia in the seventeenth century, and archaeological evidence in the form of pipes indicates that it had been used for several centuries prior to the settlement at Jamestown.

The narratives of Archer and Percy in 1607 show that tobacco had some place in the social life of the Powhatan Indians, at least to the extent that it was offered to visitors as a sign of wel-

23

come and friendship. Hamor also tells us that when he visited Powhatan at Matchot in 1614, the first thing that Powhatan did was to offer him a pipe of tobacco. However, it is very clear that the primary place of tobacco was in connection with religious rites.

Tobacco was usually grown in a plot by itself. The stalks, leaves, and all were dried in the sun, or over a fire, and crumbled to powder. It was smoked through clay or stone pipes and deeply inhaled.

The Indians believed that their gods were greatly delighted with tobacco and that it grew in the world of the dead. Smith found that they offered it to the spirits on altars, or threw it on the stormy waters to pacify their gods. Hariot tells us that the Algonquian Indians of North Carolina offered tobacco upon a newly built fish weir, or upon "hallowed fires" for a sacrifice, or cast some of it in the air after an escape from danger.

The native tobacco (*Nicotiana rustica*) was an inferior tobacco and had a "byting tast" according to Strachey. John Rolfe introduced the superior West Indian varieties which soon replaced the native tobacco, and became so popular with the English and Europeans that the colonists raised tobacco instead of the needed corn and vegetables. The better quality tobacco and the influence of the whites account no doubt for the smoking habit the Virginia Indians began to form in the early part of the seventeenth century. It is interesting to note that although the Indians used the tobacco grown by the colonists for their ordinary smoking tobacco, they continued to grow their *Nicotiana rustica* for ceremonial use.

Tobacco Pipes

Archaeological investigation has revealed several types of Virginia Indian tobacco pipes. The earliest type, usually made of clay, occasionally of stone or of bone, is often referred to as the "cloud blower" type, or as the tubular pipe since the bowl and stem form a straight line. It was probably used in some parts of the state as late as the seventeenth century.

A later type, made of clay or of soapstone, includes the slightly curved tubular pipes and those which have the bowl placed at an angle of approximately 35 or more degrees to the stem. The bowl has become somewhat larger and the stem a little longer. This type provided the model perhaps for the English and European clay pipes of commerce or "trade pipes" of the seventeenth century.

The monitor or platform pipe is frequently found in the western and southwestern parts of the state. The material from which pipes of this type were made is a chlorite or steatite. The name "monitor" suggests their general shape. They vary in length from 3 to 18 inches, with bases from 1 to 4 inches wide. The bowls are from 1 to 8 inches in depth with a diameter ranging from ¾ of an inch to 1¼ inches. This pipe was used considerably in the seventeenth century and was widely distributed in the eastern United States. It represents the finest pipe of stone found in Virginia.

Beautifully made clay pipes of late origin occur on Indian sites in Tidewater Virginia, and on colonial sites at Jamestown, Kecoughtan, and elsewhere. Viewed all together, they resemble the English trade pipes. Closer inspection shows that they are handmade of light brown to dark brown well baked clays. The paste is fine but not as fine as that of the English pipes, and the surface is smooth and often polished. There is another distinguishing characteristic: neatly punctated geometrical designs, or animal figures—usually deer—embellish the bowl and sometimes the stem.

The exact position of these pipes in the archaeological picture has not been determined, but it is believed that some of them are of Indian manufacture. If this is true, they are the finest examples of the Virginia Algonquian pipe maker's art.

Description of the Virginia Indian, Clothing of Men, Women, Children, and Priests; Bags and Purses

According to Smith, the Virginia Indians differed "Very much in stature," but were "Generally tall and straight." Strachey parallels this description, and Beverley says that they were of the "Middling and largest stature of the English." T. Dale Stewart's study of an Indian ossuary on the York River, near West Point, bears out the early accounts that the Algonquian Virginia Indians were tall. Based on a small sample of skeletal parts, but which is called typical of the area, Stewart estimated a stature of nearly six feet.

Strachey writes that the Indians were "Generally of a cullour browne or rather tawny." Their eyes were very black, and their hair was usually coal black. "The men have no beardes, their noses are broad, flatt, and full at the end, great big lippes, and wide mouths, yet nothing so unsightly as the Moores." And Beverley writes of the women: "Their women are generally beautiful, possessing an uncommon delicacy of shape and features, and wanting in no charm but that of a fair complexion."

Relative to their disposition, Smith found that they were inconstant, crafty, timorous, apprehensive, quick to anger, very ingenuous, and "Generally covetous of copper, beads, and such like trash . . . and so malitious that they seldome forget an injury."

The men's wearing apparel usually consisted of a breech-clout of skin between their thighs. The ends of the breech-clout were carried up and under the waist-cord or belt and hung down and sometimes still had attached to it the head and tail of the animal. Smith says that "The common sort have scarce to cover their nakedness but with grasse, the leaves of trees, or such like . . . The better sort use large mantels of deare skins not much differing from the Irish mantels." The skins for summer wear were dressed without the hair, fringed, and decorated with paintings

26

or beadwork representing birds and animals. For winter wear, the skins were dressed with the hair. A sort of deerskin shirt, finely dressed and fringed, was worn by the chiefs and the great men.

Mantles of turkey feathers were occasionally worn by the chiefs, and men and women of distinction. Smith says that these mantles were "So prettily wrought and woven with threeds that nothing could bee discerned but the feathers, that was exceeding warme and handsome."

The women wore a skirt which was attached at the waist and hung down in front almost to the knees, leaving their "hynder parts" almost naked. The skirt was usually made of dressed deerskin, and fringed along the upper and lower edges. The upper edge was folded over at the waist.

Strachey says that the better sort of women, for the most part, covered themselves all over with finely dressed and fringed skin mantles which were colored with designs of birds and animals. This writer also informs us that men and women wore leggings in severe weather, and as a protection from brush and briars.

Moccasins were apparently worn very little by the Indians of eastern Virginia. Beverley is the only writer to refer to them, and that is at a late date.

Girls from about the age of eight years wore a skin belt and a cord as a breech-clout which held a small bunch of moss in the front. At the age of ten or twelve years, they wore a kind of apron of dressed skin. Boys went entirely naked until they were ten or twelve years old. At that age they probably wore clothing of the kind described for girls.

The priests wore short cloaks shaped like a woman's petticoat, one end of which they tied about the shoulders, but always kept one shoulder and arm uncovered and free. The cloaks fell to about the middle of the thighs. They were occasionally made of feathers, but more frequently of a soft finely dressed skin with the fur outside.

Beverley tells us that the conjurer wore nothing but "an otter-skin at his girdle, fastening the tail between his legs." At his side hung his bag or purse. Upon one ear he wore a small black bird as a badge of his office.

An important article of the Indian male's attire was the purse or bag. Personal belongings such as tobacco, knives, flakers, pipes, etc., were carried in it. The conjurer or medicine man had particular need of the purse to carry his various medicinal roots and herbs.

The purse was worn at the right side and fastened to the belt. It was made of well dressed skin and ornamented at the lower end by a leather fringe. The Virginia Indian purse which is now preserved in the Ashmolean Museum at Oxford, England, is beautifully decorated with many tiny disc-shaped shell beads, and a few larger beads spheroid in shape. It is believed that this purse was carried to England about 1615, and it is very likely the only one extant.

ORNAMENTATION

Beads of shell, bone, copper, stone, clay, and pearls were worn by Virginia Indians in the seventeenth century. Pearls were obtained from the freshwater mussels, and from bivalves along the coast. Those of fine quality, and the beads of copper belonged primarily to the chiefs, and men and women of distinction.

Large beads were often strung on thin cord and passed several times around the neck, or wrapped around the arm as ornaments. Small shell beads were in demand for decorating purses, moccasins, belts, and other articles of clothing. Univalve *Marginella* shells were used extensively for decorating garments. Powhatan's habit, which is preserved in the Ashmolean Museum at Oxford, England, is decorated with figures of a man and two deer formed with *Marginella* shells.

Beads of shell were also used as currency in the Virginia Tidewater area before white contact. This shell money was known as roanoke (roanoak), and it probably referred to beads of several types. At least, it is evident that it applied to *Marginella* shells, and to small disc-shaped beads. The Matchipungoes became well known for their manufacture of roanoke.

An interesting example of the use of roanoke as currency is found in Ralph Hamor's narrative. When Powhatan was requested by Sir Thomas Dale, through Hamor, to send his youngest daughter to him because he wished to marry her, and also in order that she could be with her sister, Pocahontas, at Jamestown, Powhatan replied that he was unable to do this because "I have sold her within this few daies to a great werowance, for two bushels of rawrenoke (roanoke), three daies journee from me."

In the early part of the seventeenth century wampum was introduced from the north into Virginia as currency. This was a type of small cylindrical bead whose length exceeded its diameter. It averaged about a quarter of an inch in length by an eighth of an inch in diameter. It was usually made from the white and purple parts of thick clam shell or quahog *(Venus mercenaria)*. The purple wampum was given a value twice that of the white. The native wampum was soon replaced by that made by the Dutch and Swedes of the Middle States. It became very plentiful in the latter part of the seventeenth century.

The Indians made another form of shell bead called "runtees." These were made from the columella of large univalves, and they were either oval in shape or circular and flat. An unusual feature of the latter form is that it was drilled edgewise. Beads two or three inches long were made from the columella. These were greatly prized and were widely used in the state.

The most highly valued ornaments were made of copper. It seems well established that the Indians had a small source of the metal near Virgilina, Virginia. The best known major source was the Lake Superior region.

The ownership of copper was limited almost entirely to the

men and women of the better sort. Powhatan showed great avidity for copper, and whenever he visited the other werowances he expected them to present him with "copper beads or vitall." He ranked copper with good meat, women, children, comfort, and hatchets.

Native copper had to be hammered into shape because the Indians had not learned the art of smelting. Breastplates, pendants, beads, head-bands, and various ornaments for the hair and ears were made of this metal. Chains of copper, and beads were also placed on images of their god Oke, and on the bodies of their dead kings.

As soon as the English learned of the Indian's love of copper, they began to use it as an important article of trade. Copper would usually open the door for trade with Powhatan, or with the other chiefs. On one occasion, in the dead of winter, January 1609, when food was scarce, and when Powhatan did not seem disposed to trade, a copper kettle provided the stimulus and Captain Smith was able to bargain for eighty bushels of corn in exchange for it.

One of the most famous kidnappings in history was brought about by a copper kettle. In April, 1613, Captain Samuel Argall, while trading for corn at Patawomeke, induced Japazaws, werowance of the Potomacs, and his wife, by the promise of a copper kettle, to bring Pocahontas aboard the *Treasurer*, and thus was able to effect her capture.

Tattooing and Body Painting

The Indian women had an extreme fondness for tattooing elaborate designs upon their skins.

Strachey gives us the best description of tattooing of any of the early Virginia writers. He discusses the subject as follows: "The women have their armes, breasts, thighes, shoulders, and faces, cuningly ymbrodered with divers workes, for pouncing or searing their skyns with a kind of instrument heated in the fier.

They figure therein flowers and fruits of sondry lively kinds, as also snakes, serpents, eftes (beasts), etc., and this they doe by dropping uppon the seared flesh sondry coulers, which rub'd into the stampe, will never be taken away agayne, because yt will not only be dryed into the flesh, but growne therein."

Strachey's account does not make it clear that they tattooed their legs below the knees. However, Smith refers to tattooing of their legs and Percy mentions both "legges and thighes."

Hariot observes that the chief men of Roanoke were not tattooed, and that is probably true of the chief men among the Powhatan Indians. In fact, the early narratives associate tattooing with the women, and it seems likely that tattooing was not practiced a great deal on the men, or that it was limited to a few designs or identification marks raised upon the back of the shoulders.

We have no record of tattooing among the Siouan tribes of Virginia, but it was apparently done. The Cherokee of a later period practiced tattooing, and from this fact we might deduce that it was a custom of the Cherokee in Virginia of the seventeenth century.

The early narratives are not entirely clear on the subject of the use of paint among the Indian women. Beverley at a later date says that they made no use of paint but kept their skin "shining with oyl." However, Strachey informs us that the men and women smeared their bodies with "red tempered oyntments of earth" and the juice of certain roots, and that they "besmeered" themselves with it for ornamental purposes as well as to protect their bodies from mosquitoes, flies, and gnats. He adds that as a protection against summer heat and winter cold, they painted their heads and shoulders red with puccoon root crushed to a powder and mixed with walnut oil, or bear grease.

Body paint was resorted to especially by the men as a part of their preparation for war or games. The priests painted their bodies half black, half red.

Percy says of the Powhatan Indians: "Some paint their bodies blacke, some red, with artificiall knots of sundry lively colours, very beautiful and pleasing to the eye." The reference to "artificiall knots" evidently refers to tattooing.

According to Strachey, some men painted their bodies black and some yellow, "And being oyled over, they will sticke therein the soft downe of sundry couloured birdes of blewbirds, white herne shewes, and the feathers of the carnation birde . . . as if so many variety of laces were stitched to their skinns, which makes a wondrous shew; then, being angry and prepared to fight, paint and crosse their foreheadds, cheekes, and the right side of their heades diversly" (in various ways).

Red and black were evidently the favorite colors because they are referred to more frequently than the others. Yellow and white are in evidence, and blue is mentioned.

Ochrous earth provided red, yellow, or brown colors. Red puccoon was obtained from the bloodroot (*Sanguinaria canadensis*). Yellow was something provided by the yellow puccoon, or golden seal (*Hydrastis canadensis*). White earth was available in certain parts of the state and was perhaps used to provide white. Soot was certainly employed for the desirable black.

Dressing the Hair

Men and women gave considerable attention to the care of the hair. The women were the barbers for both sexes. They "grated" away the hair on the head with two shells, and used tweezers of mussel shells for plucking the hair from the body. According to Percy the married Powhatan women allowed all the hair of their heads to grow long and tied it in a long plait hanging down to their hips. The unmarried girls had the front and sides of their heads shaven close, and the hair on the back of their heads grew long and was tied in a plait which hung down the back at full length.

Hair styles of the Algonquian women of North Carolina were

32

somewhat different from those of the Virginia women. Smith's statement that the women cut their hair "In many fashions agreeable to their yeares, but ever some part remaineth long," indicates that the hair styles varied somewhat among the Powhatan women.

Flowers and feathers decorated the hair of the Powhatan women, but Swanton tells us that the use of feathers by women was not as common as the writers of idealistic prose fiction would have us believe.

The Powhatan men shaved the hair from the right side of their heads to prevent it from becoming entangled with the bowstring when they were preparing to shoot. A ridge or crown of hair like a cock's comb was retained on top of the head. The hair on the left side was allowed to grow, and, according to Percy, they wore it full length "With a lock an ell (45 inches) long" hanging down the shoulder. It was sometimes tied up in a knot which was decorated with many things, such as, the dried hand of their enemy, the whole wing of a bird with rattles tied to the feathers, shells tied loosely together, pieces of copper, etc.

Beverley says that the priests shaved all the hair off their heads except the crest on the crown and a border of hair above the forehead which "By the stiffning it receives from grease and paint, will stand out like the peak of a bonnet." The cut of the hair of the conjurers was identical to that of the priests except that the border of hair above the forehead was not retained. According to Spelman, the priests in the Potomac country shaved the hair from the right side of the head and left only a small lock at the ear and that, unlike the common people, they sometimes wore beards.

There was perhaps greater variety of hair styles among the men near the end of the seventeenth century, for Beverley writes that "The men wear their hair cut after several fashions, sometimes greas'd, and sometimes painted. The great men or better sort, preserve a long lock behind for distinction."

At the beginning of the eighteenth century, Francis Louis Michel gives us our first description of the hairdress of the Virginia Siouans (Monacan). The men had "black hair, hanging down upon their shoulders, most of them, however, have it cut short, except the women, who wear long black hair."

We have no references to the manner of hairdressing of the Virginia Iroquoian tribes of the seventeenth century.

HEAD BANDS, CROWNLETS, AND FRONTLETS

Head bands, crownlets, and frontlets of white beads, and of copper were worn by the werowances (men and women) of the Powhatan Indians. They were badges of distinction and were worn on special occasions. Other badges of distinction associated with the werowances, as well as with the important men and women, were: copper beads and pendants, earrings of pearls, cloaks, mantles, and chains of large white beads and of pearls. Large copper plates attached to the side of the head were apparently worn only by the werowances.

Strachey specifically speaks of "Their crownetts which their weroances weare" and of "frontalls of white beades, curral (probably bone or shell beads), and copper"

Percy gives a description of the head decoration of the werowance of Quiyocohannoc. He was wearing a "Crown of deares haire colloured red, in fashion of a rose fastened about his knot of haire, and a great plate of copper on the other side of his head; with two long feathers in fashion of a paire of hornes placed in the midst of his Crowne." Another reference to this kind of head decoration is found in Archer's relation. "He [king Arrohatoc] gave our Captaine [Newport] his crowne which was of deares hayre dyed redd."

The chief priest sometimes wore a very curious and distinctive headdress. It consisted of a dozen or more stuffed snake skins, skins of weasels and of many "other vermine" tied together by their tails so that they all met at the top and formed a crownlet

34

of feathers. The skins hung down about the head, neck, and shoulders of the priest and partly covered his face.

There is some evidence to indicate that near the end of the seventeenth century some of the Siouan Indians in Virginia were wearing bead crownlets.

HOUSEHOLD UTENSILS

The Virginia Powhatan Indians used wooden pots and platters for dishes. They were made of hard close-grained wood which was brought into shape by charring and scraping. Those made for the chiefs were very large. Smith makes note of being presented on one occasion with three great platters of bread. A drawing by John White, made probably 1585-1588, figures a man and woman serving themselves food from a large wooden platter.

Spoons usually held about one-half a pint, and were probably made of bison horn, or of large bivalves. Gourds of various kinds provided cups, bowls, and bottles.

Cooking pots were numerous. A high percentage of the pottery type assigned to the Late Woodland Period (see section on Prehistory of Virginia in the Appendix) extended into the Historic Period. Pottery continued to be made by the same method which had been used prior to English contact. After the clay was properly prepared it was rolled into long, thin, cylindrical strips which were superimposed spirally until the desired size and height of the vessel were obtained. Then the edges of the coils were pressed together and the vessel was made smooth on both the inside and outside. Surface treatments will be described in Appendix. Vessels of sizes, containing less than a teacup to several gallons, belonged to each household. Apparently no change in pot forms resulted from white contact, and although some English pottery was available to the Indians, they continued to use essentially their own pottery because it answered their needs and could be easily and quickly made.

The making of mortars and pestles, as in the case of pottery,

35

Representative Artifacts of the Seventeenth Century and of the Prehistoric Periods of the History of the Virginia Indians (*see* Appendix)

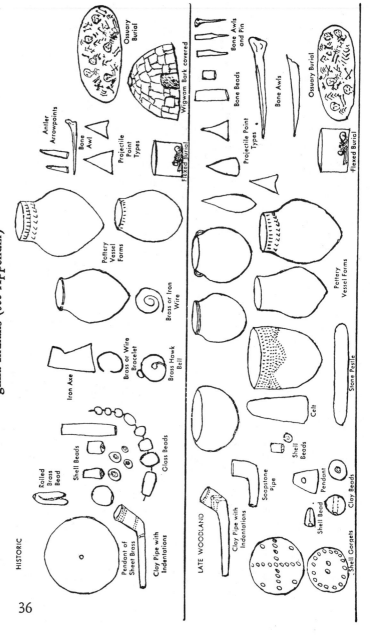

36

HISTORIC

Rolled Brass Bead

Shell Beads

Glass Beads

Pendant of Sheet Brass

Clay Pipe with Indentations

Iron Axe

Brass or Wire Bracelet

Brass Hawk Bell

Brass or Iron Wire

Pottery Vessel Forms

Anter Arrowpoints

Bone Awl

Projectile Point Types

Ossuary Burial

Wigwam Bark covered

Flexed Burial

LATE WOODLAND

Clay Pipe with Indentations

Soapstone Pipe

Shell Beads

Shell Bead

Pendant

Clay Beads

Shell Gorgets

Celt

Stone Pestle

Pottery Vessel Forms

Projectile Point Types

Bone Beads

Bone Awls and Pin

Bone Awls

Ossuary Burial

Flexed Burial

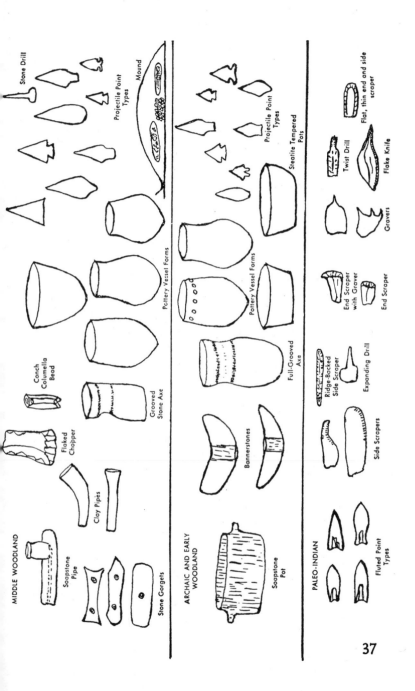

MIDDLE WOODLAND

Soapstone Pipe

Stone Gorgets

Clay Pipes

Flaked Chopper

Conch Columella Bead

Grooved Stone Axe

Pottery Vessel Forms

Projectile Point Types

Stone Drill

Mound

ARCHAIC AND EARLY WOODLAND

Soapstone Pot

Bannerstones

Full-Grooved Axe

Pottery Vessel Forms

Projectile Point Types

Steatite Tempered Pots

PALEO-INDIAN

Fluted Point Types

Side Scrapers

Ridge-Backed Side Scraper

Expanding Drill

End Scraper with Graver

End Scraper

Gravers

Twist Drill

Flake Knife

Flat, thin end and side scraper

37

was the responsibility of the women. Based on the description of these articles found elsewhere in the southeast, mortars were made from logs approximately 26 inches long by 20 inches in diameter. One end of the log was burned and scraped until a desired cavity of 10 to 14 inches deep and 14 to 18 inches wide was obtained. Pestles were commonly made of wood, probably hickory, and measured five to six feet in length. The top was broad and clubbed to provide more weight, and the end, for pounding the corn, round and slender.

Stone pestles, fifteen to twenty-odd inches in length, have been found in Virginia. These were no doubt used also for reducing corn to flour in the wooden mortars. The plentiful shallow stone mortars and small stone pestles were very likely used for crushing shells, tubers, berries, and seeds.

The women made baskets of various kinds and sizes. They were made of corn-husk, the bark of trees, wicker, native hemp, and silk grass. Twined weaving was apparently the favorite construction technique. Conical-shaped and flat bottom-shaped forms were no doubt present. Sieves of open work were used for sifting pounded corn. Spelman speaks of the hand baskets for gathering corn, and of larger baskets into which the corn was dumped. On the occasion of a visit to Opechancanough, Smith makes mention of "many women loaded with great painted baskets."

At the turn of the century (1702) there is an important reference to the baskets of the Siouan Indians of Monacantown. Michel, the Swiss traveler, refers to the large number of baskets that these people had for sale, and to the beautifully colored figures woven into them, representing animals, flowers and other strange things.

References are not numerous to this important household utensil, but they are sufficiently specific for us to conclude that very useful and pretty baskets were made by the Virginia Indians of the seventeenth century. One can imagine that the colonists

38

bought hundreds of these baskets in trade, yet not one has come down to us.

CRADLES

The cradle was apparently used to some extent by the Powhatan as well as by the Siouan Indians. Beverley, at the end of the century, gives a description of the cradle and figures it also (*History of Virginia*, 1705, bk. 3, p. 9). "The first thing they do, is to dip the child over head and ears in cold water, and then to bind it naked to a convenient board, having a hole fitly plac'd for evacuation; but they always put cotton, wool, furr, or other soft thing, for the body to rest easy on, between the child and the board."

The board was flat and about two feet long by one foot wide. A leather strap extending from one upper corner to the other made it easy to hang it up, or for the mother to carry it on her back. The child remained fastened to the board for several months.

IMPLEMENTS AND WEAPONS

Very excellent knives were made, according to Smith of "the splinter of a reed" with which the Indian could "Cut his feathers in forme. With this knife also, he will joint a deare or any beast, shape his shoes, buskins, mantels, etc." Stone chips or "flake knives" and shells appear to have served as knives in late as well as in earlier periods. Trade knives of metal became more available to the Indians as the seventeenth century moved on.

The incisor of a beaver set in a bone or wooden handle was a useful implement for executing the secondary flaking on stone implements, or for fine work on wood or bone. This tool in association with the bone handle has been recovered on several sites in Virginia.

Early historic sites have yielded many implements of bone. They were manufactured from deer antler, deer bones, bird bones, especially those of the turkey, and included such items

39

as: pins, awls, flakers, fish-hooks, arrowpoints, spearpoints for fishing, and chisels.

Other important implements were scrapers of bone, stone, and shell, and drills of stone, and reed. All the above objects were gradually replaced by trade implements of metal.

The axe referred to in the early narratives was perhaps the celt. This type of stone tool rather than the grooved axe appears on late sites. It was hafted by thrusting it tightly into a hole prepared in a handle of wood. Glue was used to hold it more firmly in place. The horn of a deer hafted in the same manner served as an implement of war.

Curved swords, about three feet long, of tough heavy wood which was sometimes ornamented with paintings and engraved designs, were carried by the Indians. Percy speaks of another type of sword "Beset with sharpe stone, and pieces of yron able to cleave a man in sunder." English hatchets and axes of iron rapidly replaced the Indian axe.

Bows were the important implement of hunt as well as of war. Much labor and care were involved in their manufacture. They were made of various kinds of wood, but specific mention is made of witch-hazel and locust wood. Smith says that "They bring their bowes to the forme of ours by the scraping of a shell." They were usually from five to six feet in length.

There are three Virginia Indian bows now preserved in the Ashmolean Museum at Oxford, England, which were sent over from Virginia about 1615. The wood resembles ash, and their lengths are approximately, five feet three inches, five feet seven inches, and five feet nine inches. Bowstrings were made of stag's gut, deer sinew, or a strip of deer-hide twisted tightly.

Two types of arrows are described by the early writers. One was made of a wooden shaft tipped with a bone two or three inches in length, and it was used chiefly for shooting squirrels and birds. The other type of arrow had a reed shaft and a wooden-foreshaft. It was tipped with the spur of a turkey, the bill of some bird, the tine of an antler, or an arrowpoint of stone. The stone projectile point was likely of the small triangular type which predominates on late sites in Virginia. The point was adjusted to a split in the foreshaft and bound tightly by means of glue and sinew.

The arrows were feathered with split turkey feathers which were bound to the shaft with a glue made from the tips of deer horns boiled to a jelly. The early accounts do not make it clear whether the Virginia Indians of the seventeenth century used two or three feathers on the shaft. At a much later date, some Indians of the southeast used two feathers and some used three.

There is some reason to believe that the Virginia Indians occasionally used poisoned arrows. The *Relation of the Discovery*, attributed to Captain Gabriel Archer, says, "One gave me a roote wherewith they poison their arrowes" (Smith, John, *Works*, Arber ed., 1910).

An essential part of the Indian's accoutrements was his flaker. It was usually made of deer antler, and was from four to five inches long by one-half to an inch thick. With this tool an arrowhead of stone could be quickly flaked into shape, or a broken point reworked without its removal from the shaft.

The flaker was always worn on the bracer or wrist-guard which, according to Strachey, was "Commonly made of some beast's skynne, eyther of the woolf, badger, or black fox, etc."

Quivers were made in most cases of skin, but rushes and bark were also used. Circular shields of bark were sometimes worn for defense. Spelman informs us that they were "Hanged on ther leaft shoulder to cover that side as they stand forth to shoote." The shields were occasionally painted red.

Relative to the effectiveness of the bow and arrow, Smith says: "Forty yards will they shoot levell, or very neare the mark, and 120 is their best at random." Percy tells about an interesting experiment made to test the force of the Indian arrows: "One of our gentlemen having a target [shield] which hee trusted in,

41

thinking it would beare out a slight shot, hee set it up against a tree, willing one of the savages to shoot: who tooke from his backe an arrow of an elle [45 inches] long, drew it strongly in his bowe, shoots the target a foote thorow, or better: which was strange, being that a pistoll could not pierce it. Wee seeing the force of his bowe, afterwards set him up a steel target: he shot again, and burst his arrow all to pierces."

Firearms did not replace the bow and arrow as rapidly as the iron and steel trade knives and axes replaced the aboriginal knives and axes. This was due to some extent to the laws enacted during the first half of the seventeenth century prohibiting the trading of guns and ammunition to the Indians. But these laws began to break down because the neighboring "plantations both English and forrainers" (the Dutch) were selling firearms to the Virginia Indians. During most of the last quarter of the century, free and open trade was permitted with all friendly Indians.

Methods of Warfare

The weapons used in warfare by the Powhatan Indians consisted of bows and arrows and clubs. Shields were occasionally used to provide some protection.

When the great werowance intended to wage war he called together a council of his subject werowances, trusted counselors, friends, allies, priests and conjurers. The words of powerful leaders like Powhatan and Opechancanough carried great weight in the council, but Strachey tells us that the priests had "The resulting voice, and determyne therefore their resolutions." After war had been determined upon, a werowance or some lusty fellow was appointed captain over "A nation or regiment to be led forth" and no one dared to refuse to serve the great king when an officer was sent to notify him to be present.

It is evident that Powhatan waged his wars principally to satisfy his craving for power. His brother, Opechancanough, fought two wars in an attempt to drive the English out of the country. However, Strachey makes a statement that explains the causes of the greater number of wars the Algonquians fought among themselves, as well as with their hereditary enemies the Siouans. He says: "They seldome make warrs for lands or goods, but for women and children, and principally for revenge, so vindicative and jealous they be to be made a dirision of, and to be insulted upon by an enemy."

In order to be prepared and to be successful, the Indians engaged in mimic warfare, or war games. When they went into actual battle, they wore only the breech-clout, but painted their bodies in every manner they could devise.

They chiefly resorted to surprise and treachery to insure victory. Powhatan used both very effectively to destroy the Piankatank, his neighbors and subjects, in 1608. He sent a few of his men to lodge with them one night on the pretense of a general hunt. When the Piankatank were asleep, these men signaled a larger number of warriors hiding in the forest around the village, and the massacre followed. Only a few men escaped, and the women and children, and the werowance were presented to Powhatan. The scalps of the men killed were taken to Werowocomoco and hung on a line stretched between two trees, and pointed out to the English traders, hoping to terrify them by such a spectacle.

The war against the Chesapeake Indians provided a good example of the power of the priests, who had prophesied to Powhatan that a great people would arise and come in from the east through the Chesapeake Bay. Thereupon, Powhatan waged a war upon those people and practically destroyed them because of his faith in his priests and his fear of anyone in that region.

The Powhatan Indians never fought in open fields, but concealed themselves behind reeds, tall grass, or trees, and watched for an opportunity to shoot at the enemy. If they wounded him they would rush upon him and kill him with their clubs. Those who killed the greatest number of the enemy were considered

"The cheafest men amonge them," according to Spelman. And he adds that during the fight "They have a kind of howlinge or howbabub so differinge in sounde one from the other as both part may very aesely be distinguished."

In order to prevent discovery when they were on the march, or to make it difficult for the enemy to follow them after a battle, they would separate each morning and agree to meet at an appointed place.

The methods of fighting of the Siouan and Iroquoian groups in Virginia in the seventeenth century were probably similar in many respects to those of the Powhatan.

Artistic Efforts

The Virginia Indians had begun to develop some art appreciation before the coming of the whites, and it is manifested in several ways. We find references in the early literature to the images of their kings and devils placed in the "chief holy house" near Uttamussack, at Pamunkey. These images were crudely carved, painted black, and decorated with chains of copper, pearls, and beads.

Beverley speaks of posts, with faces carved on them and painted, which were placed "round about" the temples. Posts with men's faces carved upon them and painted, were set up in a circle at other "celebrated places" and the people gathered and danced around them on "certain solemn occasions."

Smith provides an example of other carved figures which were set up at Powhatan's treasure house at Orapaks. "At the four corners of this house stand four images as sentinels, one of a dragon, another of a beare, the third like a leopard, and the fourth like a giantlike man: all made evill favordly, according to their best workmanship."

It is probable that certain designs were woven into the baskets, and into a few household mats, although the earliest writers refer to them as painted articles. If we can believe Francis Louis

Michel, the Swiss traveler who was in Virginia in 1701-2, the Siouan Indians at Monacantown were weaving into their baskets "all kinds of animals, flowers, and other strange things, very beautifully."

We have one example in Powhatan's habit, already mentioned, of designs in beadwork on wearing apparel.

Indian village sites of the historic period have produced durable objects of bone, stone, and clay, which were artistically shaped and decorated.

Soapstone pipes of the elbow type have been found in the Piedmont, in the northern and southwestern parts of the state, which have figures of men and animals etched on the bowl. A few small carved stone faces have been recovered. These probably represent the efforts of Siouan Indians. Pottery pipes from the Tidewater area have come to light exhibiting animal figures and symbols carefully outlined on the bowl by finely placed indentations.

Pottery vessels of the late period occasionally show some artistic attempt by the use of incised decorative lines around the rim.

Historic sites have produced shell gorgets having designs made by the drilled-dot technique. Elaborate symbolical designs often in the form of a snake are sometimes found on shell gorgets from the southwestern part of the state.

Musical Instruments

The musical instruments of the Virginia Indians were limited to drums, rattles, and flutes or flageolets. Rattles were made of gourds and pumpkins, and constituted their most important musical instrument. Smith says that, "Of these they have base, tenor, countertenor, meane and trible." They were used to accompany the singing and dancing that took place on important occasions around the fire, or the circle of carved poles.

Drums of the early part of the seventeenth century were made of a wooden platter covered with a tightly drawn skin, and follow-

45

ing Smith's description, at each corner they tied "A walnut, which meeting on the backside neere the bottome, with a small rope they twitch them togither till it be so tought and stiffe, that they may beat upon it as upon a drumme." Smith and Strachey speak of the drum only as an instrument used in war. However, Beverley, at the end of the century, places the drum among the musical instruments, and we find that the method of manufacture is different from that described by the early writers. Beverley writes: "Their musical instruments are chiefly drums and rattles: Their drums are made of a skin stretched over an earthen pot half full of water."

The flageolet, precursor of the modern flute, is one of the oldest musical instruments known to man. It was found not only in Virginia but over much of the southeast. Smith describes it briefly: "For their musicke they use a thicke cane, on which they pipe as on a recorder." In writing of the visit in May 1607, paid the Rapahanna (Quiyocohannoc), Percy says that "The werowance of Rapahanna came downe to the water side with all his traine, as goodly men as any I have seene of savages or Chistians: the werowance comming before them playing on a flute made of a reed."

GAMES

The Algonquian Indians along the seaboard, as well as most of the southern Indians, played a game very similar to lacrosse. As a matter of fact, we are told that the French-Canadian settlers borrowed the game from the Indians and modified it. The southern Indians used two sticks. Each had a loop at the end to which was attached a little corded cage in which the ball was caught. Two groups representing a town, or a tribe, played against each other, and each side had a goal to which it tried to carry the ball. A reference by Strachey apparently refers to this game: "A kynd of exercise they have often amongst them much like that which boyes call bandy [hockey] in England."

The Powhatan Indians were fond of football. Only the foot

could be used to move the ball toward the goal. It required a great deal of speed and dexterity on the part of the player.

Spelman seems to indicate that there was a football game for men, and one for women: "They use beside football play which wemen and young boyes doe much play at. The men never. They make their gooles as ours only they never fight nor pull one another doune.

"The men play with a litel balle lettinge it fall out of ther hand and striketh it with the tope of his foot, and he that can strike the ball furthest winns that they play for."

There is reason to believe that the Cherokee Indians in Virginia during the seventeenth century played some kind of ball, because we find that in the following century it had such an important place in their social and ceremonial life.

The game called chunkey was widespread in the southeast. The early travelers' descriptions of the game lead us to believe that there were some differences in the game but basically it was the same everywhere. It was played with a disc-shaped stone roller and slender poles eight or ten feet long. The finest stone material was selected for the stone roller or discoidal, and a great deal of time and care were required to bring it to the required shape. It measured three to five inches in diameter and approximately one and one-quarter inches in thickness. There were usually only two players in the game, and the object was to roll the discoidal along a carefully prepared flat, smooth piece of ground, and each player was to throw his pole to either hit the roller, or to place his pole as near as possible to the place where the roller came to rest. Each player could also try to throw his pole in such a way as to deflect that of his opponent from its intended mark.

There is no mention in the early narratives of chunkey in Virginia. Its place in the life of the Virginia Indians was perhaps small, but they knew the game and played it to a certain extent because chunkey stones have been found in widely scattered counties in the state. The latest reported was found in Charles City County.

Round stone balls from one to two and one-half inches in diameter have been recovered in various parts of the state, and many egg-shaped stones slightly less than two inches in diameter have occurred on Indian sites around the Dismal Swamp area. Both forms were probably used in some kind of "rolling the stone" game.

A kind of game in which small sticks were used is described by Beverley: "They have also one great diversion, to the practising of which are requisite whole handfuls of sticks or hard straws, which they know how to count as fast as they can cast their eyes upon them, and can handle with a surprising dexterity."

Strachey describes a very similar game: "Dice play, or cardes, or lotts they knowe not, how be it they can use a game upon russhes much like primero [a game at cards from which modern poker is derived], wherein they card and discard, and lay a stake too, and so win and loose. They will play at this for their bowes and arrowes, their copper beads, hatchets, and their leather coats."

Round pottery and stone discs from one-half an inch to two inches in diameter are frequently found on sites in the southwestern part of the state, in the Cherokee country, and they may have served as counters in some kind of game employing simple arithmetic.

In addition to the games described above, Beverley says that they engaged in "Some boisterous plays, which are perform'd by running, catching and leaping upon one another."

MARRIAGE CUSTOMS

Most of the information that we have relative to the marriage customs of the Virginia Indians comes from the pen of Spelman, and that applies only to the Powhatans.

Spelman tells us that it was the custom among the Indians for a man to have as many wives as he could afford. The man with the most copper and beads could have the greatest number of wives. Actually, polygamy was limited for the most part to a few great men, and to the werowances who could support more than one wife.

If a man found a woman to his liking, he courted her and arranged the price with her father, or relatives. When the price was agreed upon, the relatives of both parties met and made good cheer. After the price was paid the woman was brought to the man by her parents, or by someone appointed. At her arrival, her father or a close friend placed her hands in those of her future husband. Then the father or a close friend of the man took a string of beads, and after measuring an arm's length, broke it over the joined hands of the couple, and gave it to the woman's father or to the person who had brought her. After this ceremony much mirth and feasting followed.

Strachey gives us some general information on the subject of marriage. He tells us that the man expressed his interest in the girl he wanted to be his wife by presenting her with game, fish, fowl, fruits, and berries to impress her with his ability as a hunter and provider. When the young girl reached marriageable age, the parents had to permit the young man to press his suit; and to incline them in his favor, he promised to always procure for her, food, deer skins, beads, pearls, and copper, and gave her in the presence of her parents a token of betrothal or a contract of further amity and acquaintance. Then the marriage would follow as soon as the man had provided a house, platters, mortars, and mats.

When Powhatan wanted wives he informed his chief men of it, and they went into all parts of the country to find the fairest maids. He selected those who pleased him, and gave their parents any price he wished. Strachey says that Powhatan had more than a hundred wives.

A werowance never had but one child by the same wife. At the birth of the child, the wife left the household of the werowance, but he gave her sufficient copper and beads to provide for all her needs. When the child reached a certain age, it was taken from the mother and placed in the charge of the werowance. Henceforth, the mother was free to marry again.

Marriage was considered sacred, and divorce was frowned upon. Infidelity was considered the most unpardonable of crimes. When separation did take place, all ties of matrimony were considered dissolved and each party was free to marry another. In these separations, if difference arose over the division of the children, they were divided equally, and the man was given the first choice.

DIVISION OF WORK BETWEEN THE SEXES

The men and women had numerous and various tasks to perform in their society, and these tasks were rather sharply divided.

The men spent the greater part of their time in hunting, fishing and making war. They made all the implements necessary for these endeavors, such as, bows and arrows, shields, tomahawks, weirs, etc. Other tasks which fell to the men were: the felling of trees and the making of dugout canoes, preparation of the fields for corn and of the gardens, the building of the more permanent houses, the making of ceremonial objects, and holding the ceremonies. The youths helped to a certain extent in making bows and arrows and in repairing the necessary ceremonial objects. These tasks required much time, and called for great expenditure of energy, yet they allowed the men some periods of rest, or even of idleness.

The women, on the other hand, had so many duties that their work was never done. They had to gather the wood, make the fire, prepare the food, cook it, and serve it. They made the pots, mats, baskets, and mortars, planted the corn, cared for the garden, gathered the corn, and pounded it in the mortars. They did much of the housebuilding, kept the dwelling in repair, carried the mats and built temporary shelters for the hunters. They dressed skins, made the clothing and kept it in repair. The women, with the help of the old men, taught the boys to shoot. Fortunately, the girls took care of the younger children, and in their spare moments, helped with the sewing or other urgent handwork.

The few women who had no tasks to perform were the favorite wives of the werowance, and the women werowances. They were treated with great respect and waited upon by servants.

Burial Customs

It is not known to what extent the single burial form was practiced among the Virginia Algonquians. Smith gives us the following description: "For their ordinary burials they digge a deep hole in the earth with sharpe stakes; and the corp(s)es being lapped in skins and mats with their jewels, they lay them upon sticks in the ground, and so cover them with earth. The buriall ended, the women being painted all their faces with black cole and oile, doe sit 24 howers in the houses mourning and lamenting by turnes, with such yelling and howling as may expresse their great passions."

Several interesting burial traits are noted in the preceding passage. We learn that some care was given to the preparation of the corpse for burial; grave goods were placed with the body; and those mourning the dead blackened their faces with charcoal.

Spelman says that when a man died the body was wrapped in mats and placed on a scaffold ten or twelve feet above ground. The relatives gathered there moaned and wept, and, as a part of the ceremony, threw beads among the poor. Later the company went to the house of the relatives of the dead, and spent the remainder of the day in feasting, singing and dancing. After the flesh had disappeared entirely from the bones, they were taken from the scaffold, wrapped in a new mat, placed in a house and left there until the house fell in. Then they were buried in the ruins of the house.

Among the burial traits noted in Spelman's account is that

51

of the secondary burial. This form was practiced widely in the eastern part of the United States.

The Powhatan Indians developed a rather specialized burial practice for their kings or werowances. Smith and Strachey give very similar accounts of this practice, and we shall quote only from the former: "Their bodies are first bowelled, then dryed upon hurdles till they bee verie dry, and so about the most of their jointes and necke they hang bracelets or chaines of copper, pearle, and such like, as they used to weare: their inwards they stuffe with copper beads and cover with a skin, hatchets, and such trash. Then lappe they them very carefully in white skins, and so rowle them in mats for their winding sheetes. And in the tombe, which is an arch made of mats, they lay them orderly. What remaineth of this kinde of wealth their kings have, they set at their feet in baskets. These temples and bodies are kept by their priests."

The tomb which Smith describes as "An arch made of mats," was a raised platform with a top and side covering of mats prepared within the temples or ossuaries. In this place they also set up images of their deities to guard the dead.

Archaeological investigation has revealed that the reburial method in pits or ossuaries was practiced in Tidewater Virginia in the seventeenth century. Ossuaries found along the Potomac, Rappahannock, and York rivers have been carefully examined. They show the following features: saucer-shaped pits, bones deposited in bundles, some burial goods, a small quantity of burnt bones, evidence of dental caries, and according to T. D. Stewart, of the United States National Museum, the presence of syphilitic bones. The significance of burnt bones in the pits is not clear, but it has been suggested that the cremation of one or more individuals was part of the burial ceremony.

It is possible that some of the bodies in the pits were primary interments, but certain evidences found with the skeletal parts, and the manner in which they were deposited make it clear that most of them represent secondary burials.

A number of the pits found in the area mentioned yielded European trade goods which evidently dates them after 1607.

We have no descriptions of the burial customs during the seventeenth century in the remaining area of the state. In the north, central, and southern parts of Virginia, there was almost constant movement of the population. Very little contact was made with the tribes west of the falls, and by the time the whites were entering that region the Siouans had gone. Pressure from hostile tribes on the north had forced them to move into North Carolina.

Various methods of disposal of the dead can be observed in this large area. Burial mounds are found in the Piedmont, but the greatest concentration is west of the Blue Ridge. These burial mounds belong to the prehistoric period for the most part, and reflect probably an intrusion of the mound complex from the Ohio and West Virginia areas. A few stone graves occur in western Virginia. Cave burials are noted in the southwest, in the limestone area. They may prove to be a local burial trait of the Cherokee Indians of that section. Examples of individual burials, in flexed and occasionally extended positions, in or near the village sites are found throughout the state.

The Virginia Siouan tribes in the seventeenth century probably had burial customs similar to the Siouans of North Carolina of a later date. According to Lawson they had preburials on scaffolds, accompanied by formalized orations in the presence of relatives and friends. Then followed the secondary burial which involved placing the body in a kind of wooden vault prepared in the earth. After the flesh had disappeared the bones were collected and if the relatives could pay the admittance charge, the bones were placed in the royal tomb or burial place. If the Indians moved, they carried all the bones of the dead with them.

Another interesting mortuary trait that Lawson mentions is that the relatives of the great men paid professional mourners to cry and lament over the dead.

CRIME AND PUNISHMENT

The chiefs among the Virginia Algonquians had the power of life and death over their subjects and the people dared not disobey to the slightest extent. The kind of punishment varied according to the kind of offense.

In the Potomac country convictions of murder, stealing of copper, beads, corn, and adultery were punished with death. Spelman, an eye-witness to the punishment, describes it: "Then cam the officer to thos that should dye, and with a shell cutt of[f] ther long locke, which they weare on the left side of ther heade, and hangeth that on a bowe before the kings house. Then thos for murther wear beaten with staves till ther bonns weare broken and beinge alive weare flounge into the fier, the other for robbinge was knockt on the heade and beinge deade his bodye was burnt."

Relative to stealing, Smith says that the Indians seldom stole from each other because they were afraid their conjurers could reveal it.

Powhatan was very terrible in his wrath and methods of punishment. A very realistic account of Powhatan's manner of punishment is given by Smith: "For example, hee caused certaine malefactors to be bound hand and foot, then having of many fires gathered great store of burning coles, they rake these coles round in the forme of a cockpit, and in the midst they cast the offenders to broyle to death. Sometimes he causeth the heads of them that offend him to be laid upon the altar or sacrificing stone, and one with clubbes beates out their braines. When he would punish any notorious enimie or malefactor, he causeth him to be tied to a tree, and with muscle shels or reeds, the executioner cutteth of[f] his joints one after another, ever casting what they cut of[f] in the fire; then doth he proceed with shels and reeds to case the skinne from his head and face; then doe they rip his belly, and so burne him with the tree and all. Thus themselves reported they executed George Cassen.

"Their ordinary correction is to beate them with cudgels. Wee have seene a man kneeling on his knees; and at Powhatan's command, two men have beat him on the bare skin, till he hath fallen senselesse in a s[w]ound, and yet never cry nor complained."

Other examples of "ordinary correction" are found in the early narratives. If a guard failed in his duty, Powhatan had severe corporal punishment inflicted upon him. King Pasptanses, in a rage on one occasion, almost killed one of his wives because, during his absence, she had beaten Spelman, the English boy who was living with him. King Arahatec, during a visit paid him by the English, soundly whipped one of his men because he had roughly shoved against an Englishman.

Beverley provides us with an example, later in the century, of extreme punishment that was meted out by a werowance to one of his subjects because he presumed to interrupt the werowance: "In the time of Bacon's Rebellion, one of these werowances, attended by several others of his nation, was treating with the English in New Kent County, about a peace; and during the time of his speech, one of his attendants presum'd to interrupt him, which he resented as the most unpardonable affront that cou'd be offer'd him, and therefore he instantly took his tomahawk from his girdle, and split the fellow's head, for his presumption. The poor fellow dying immediately upon the spot, he commanded some of his men to carry him out, and went on again with his speech where he left off, as unconcern'd as if nothing had happen'd."

We have no seventeenth century account of the methods of punishment used by the Virginia Siouans. Later accounts of the Siouan tribes of North Carolina, might reflect their earlier customs in Virginia. The North Carolina Siouans, according to Lawson, treated murder by retaliation. A man found guilty of poisoning others was killed and his body cut to pieces. Incest was punishable by death, and the offender's body burned and the ashes thrown into the river.

The Virginia Cherokee chiefs of the seventeenth century probably did not have the arbitrary power of a Powhatan, if we can judge of this by their customs at a much later date. The Cherokee chiefs could not inflict punishment, the council and not the chiefs handled this matter.

Religious Beliefs

The early writers do not give as much information on the religious beliefs of the Virginia Indians as would be expected. Several reasons for this insufficiency are apparent. The English had little opportunity to gather first-hand knowledge because of the secret nature of the religion. The priests, and conjurers, the guardians of the temples and experts in matters of religion, did not wish to reveal the secrets of their professions. Furthermore, the English could find nothing to admire in the polytheistic and idolatrous religion of the heathens to whom they were primarily interested in teaching their own Christian religion. However, the writings of Smith, Strachey, Spelman, and Beverley, and scattered statements in the early narratives of several other writers do provide some comprehension of the religion of the Algonquian tribes of Virginia. At any rate, there is sufficient information to impress upon us the fact that religion played a very important role in the life of the Indian.

Every territory of a werowance had a temple (quioccosan). The building was in the form of an arbor, loaf-shaped, and was 18 to 20 feet wide and 30 to 100 feet long. The door faced east, and in the west end was a sort of chancel, partitioned from the main body of the building by mats. Within this special apartment, a platform several feet high contained the bodies of the dead werowances. Within the chancel also was the image of their god Okee or Okeus "Ill-favoredly carved, all black dressed, with chains of pearls." Some temples contained several of these images. Smith tells us that an image of the Okeus was sometimes carried by war parties.

Placed also within the temple and occasionally within the chancel were wooden posts with the upper portions carved to resemble human heads and faces and painted black "With their faces looking down the church." These posts were effigies of their dead chiefs.

Chief Powhatan's principal temple was at Uttamussack, probably situated on the east side of the Pamunkey River within the present Pamunkey Indian Reservation. Seven priests usually resided there. Near the temple were three large supplementary buildings "Filled with images of their kings and divels and tombes of their predecessors." The place was considered so holy that only the kings and priests dared enter there. When the people passed by it, going up or down the river, they would solemnly cast "Some peece of copper, white beads or pocones into the river for feare their Okee should be offended and revenged of them."

The ordinary temple was in charge of one, two, and sometimes three priests who kept a perpetual fire near the eastern end. A werowance considered himself fortunate if he could detain with him, a quiyoughquisock who was serious, well instructed in the mysteries of the religion, and beloved of the god.

Smith informs us that the inferior priests could hardly be distinguished from the common people, "But that they had not so many holes in their eares to hang their jewels at." The head-dress of the chief priests, already described, with its cluster of skins of snakes, weasels, etc., would easily identify them.

Both Hariot and Smith indicate a distinction among the priests. There were the chief priests and the inferior priests. The chief priests were apparently older and more experienced. The conjurer or wonder workers belonged for the most part to the class of inferior priests.

The priests had great power over the people, as well as over the werowances, and Beverley and later writers tell us that the priests continued to wield this great power during the seventeenth century. The credulous people were told by the priests that their god Okee, or Okeus, was responsible for all the evil in the world, and that in order to appease this god, they must make sacrifices as instructed by the priests, even though children or strangers were involved. The people were taught also that the great god Ahone was responsible for all the good in their lives, that he governed the world, and as Strachey describes it, "Makes the sun to shine, creating the moone and starrs his companyons, great powers, and which dwell with him, and by whose virtues and influences the under earth is tempered, and brings forth her fruicts according to her seasons." No sacrifice had to be made to this good and peaceful god, because he would do the people no harm. But Okeus required the sacrifices determined by the priests, because "The displeased Okeus, looking into all men's accions, and examining the same according to the severe scale of justice, punisheth them with sicknesses, beats them and strikes their ripe corn with blastings, stormes, and thunderclapps, stirrs up warre, and makes their women falce unto them."

Spelman gives us an account of the power of the priests in the Potomac country. If the people wanted rain, or had too much, they offered beads, and copper to the images of their god Quioquascacke, "but upon necessity," once a year, the priests or conjurers met with the men, women, and children in the woods where the priests made a great fire. After "Many observances in ther conjurations they made offer of 2 or 3 children to be given to ther god if he will apeare unto them and shew his mind whome he [will have] desier." As soon as the offer had been made, a voice would appear to come out of the circle of the fire announcing the name of those to be sacrificed, "For be it the Kinges sonne he must be given if once named by ther god."

The priests or conjurers were called upon by the people or by the chiefs to obtain knowledge of the future by divinations. Smith describes a conjuration or conjuring ceremony which concerned him, and which he had to witness for three or four days while he was a prisoner of Powhatan. Its purpose was to determine if any more of Smith's "Countrymen would arive there, and what he there intended."

Two passages in the early narratives refer to the reverence the Powhatan Indians had for the sun. In the *Relation* ascribed to Archer, we are told that in their meeting with Powhatan at the falls in June 1607, the English spoke of their encounter with the Chesapeake Indians and of their hurts "For which we vowed revenge, after their manner, pointing to the sunne."

Percy tells us that when the English, on one occasion, restored a canoe, to the king of Rapahanna, "[He] lifted up his hand to the sunne (which they worship as their God), besides he laid his hand on his heart, that he would be our speciall friend. It is a generall rule of these people when they swere by their God which is the sunne, no Christian will keep their oath better upon this promise. These people have a great reverence to the sunne above all other things: at the rising and the setting of the same, they sit downe lifting up their hands and eyes to the sunne, making a round circle on the ground with dried tobacco; then they began to pray, making many devillish gestures, with a hellish noise, foming at the mouth, staring with their eyes, wagging their heads and hands in such a fashion and deformitie as it was monstrous to behold."

The Powhatan Indians' worship of the sun was probably in the same category as their worship of any great force in nature, such as, fire, lightning, thunder, and water. Smith says they even worshiped "Our ordinance, peeces, horses, etc."

Concerning immortality of the soul, Smith records that "They think that their werowances and priestes, which they also esteeme Quiyoughcosughes, when they are dead, doe goe beyound the mountaines towardes the setting of the sun, and ever remaine there in forme of their Oke, with their heads painted with oile and pocones, finely trimmed with feathers; and shal have beads, hatchets, copper, and tobacco, doing nothing but dance and sing with all their predecessors." Strachey parallels Smith's account and adds, "Till that [they] waxe old there, as the body did on earth, and then it shall dissolve and die, and come into a woman's womb againe, and so be a new borne unto the world."

According to Smith and Strachey, the Virginia Algonquians did not believe that the common people would live after death.

Altar stones called pawcorances were erected near their houses or in the woods to commemorate some extraordinary encounter or accident. The history of their erection was passed on from generation to generation. Upon these they offered deer-suet, blood, and tobacco when they returned from their wars, from their hunting, and on many other occasions.

Beverley says that the Indians had a profound respect for these altars, and he describes one in particular for which many of their nation had great veneration: "There also was [at Uttamussack] their great pawcorance, or altar-Stone, which the Indians tell us, was a solid chrystal, of between three and four foot cube, upon which, in their greatest solemnities, they used to sacrifice. This they would make us believe, was so clear, that the grain of a man's skin might be seen through it; and was so heavy too, that when they remov'd their gods and kings, not being able to carry it away, they buried it thereabouts: but the place has never been yet discover'd."

The Indians apparently did not keep any day more holy than the other, but they gathered for religious ceremonies on any occasion of great distress, want, fear, or triumph. They celebrated also at harvest time. In the latter part of the seventeenth century, according to Beverley, they had feasts associated with the seasons. There was one for the coming of the wild fowl, for the return of their hunting season, and for the ripening of certain fruits. Their greatest feast was at the time of their corn-gathering, to which were devoted several days of sports, of singing, and dancing.

Smith describes their social gatherings and dances: "The whole country of men and women and children come togither to solemnities. The manner of their devotion is sometimes to make a great fire in the house or fields, and all to sing and dance about it, with rattles and shouts togither, 4 or 5 houres. Sometimes they set a man in the midst, and about him they dance and sing; he all the while clapping his hands as if he would keepe time. And after their songs and dauncings ended, they goe to their feasts."

Spelman, who no doubt witnessed the dances, says that first a man then a woman entered the dance, "And so through them all, hanging all in a round." And Strachey tells us that a man stood near the dancers beating the time on "Some furre or leather thing in his leaft hand," that the dancers entered the circle one at a time and danced an equal distance from each other. They kept "stroak" or time with their feet, "But with the hands, head, face and body, every one hath a severall gesture; and who have seene the darvises, in their holy daunces, in their moscas, upon Wendsedays and Frydayes in Turkey, maye resemble these unto them."

No great effort to convert the natives to Christianity was being made even as late as the last quarter of the seventeenth century, if we can rely upon the remarks of a traveler in Virginia in 1686 (see *A Huguenot Exile in Virginia,* ed. Gilbert Chinard, New York, 1934). The traveler visited an Indian settlement which stood on the right bank of the Rappahannock River, probably on the eastern shore of Port Tobago Bay, on the site of the Nandtaughtacund village of 1608, and found that "The ministers in this country take no pains to convert them to Christianity or to instruct them, although most of them know how to speak English." He also tells us that the Indians had a very imperfect knowledge of the true God, and that they were not so much concerned with Him as they were with the inferior demons who were created to abuse them.

Beverley's observations concerning the religion of the Indians are similar in most respects to those of the early writers. The Indians believed in an eternal, perfect, and benevolent god, and that all good things flowed naturally and promiscuously from him. Therefore, it was to no purpose to worship or fear him. On the contrary, it was necessary to pacify the evil spirit, to adore him, to make sacrifices to him, or he would take away all the good things that the good spirit had given them. The priests, who still wielded great power, were now teaching that the souls of all men survived their bodies and that there was an *Elizium* for them where was stored the highest perfection of earthly pleasures. There was also a hell or filthy stinking lake where the wicked went after death, and where they were tormented day and night "With furies in the shape of old women."

The accounts we have of the religion of the Virginia Siouan and Iroquoian groups are based on observations made in the early part of the eighteenth century, at a time when the Indian religion had been influenced and changed somewhat by the Christian religion. Even at this date, however, the structure of the Siouan religion resembles that of the Virginia Algonquian.

THE HUSKANAW

There is one religious rite of the Virginia Algonquians which apparently interested the early writers because they describe it rather fully.

Smith and Strachey speak of it as a "sacrifice of children" which was made once a year and whose purpose was twofold: to subject boys to a severe test in order to determine if they should be trained for the priesthood, and to make a sacrifice to their god Okee and other gods.

The strange ceremony was reserved for fifteen promising boys between ten and fifteen years of age. In the morning of the first day of the ceremony, the boys were painted white and brought forth. The people danced and sang about them with rattles until the afternoon. At that time, the children were placed at the foot of a tree around which stood a guard of the ablest of the men, each "Having a bastinado in his hand made of reeds bound together." Then the guards formed a lane, through which five appointed young men were to run to "fetch those children."

Each young man ran in turn through the lane and brought back a child, and as he ran the guards rained unmerciful blows upon his body with which he protected the child.

During this time, the women were looking on from a distance, crying out, and weeping. After the children had been carried through the double row of guards, the latter tore the tree completely apart and made garlands for their heads of its branches and leaves. The children were then "cast on a heap in a valley, as dead," and a great and solemn feast was prepared there for the whole company.

The colonists were never permitted to witness the rest of the ceremony. However, according to Smith's account "The werowance being demanded the meaning of this sacrifice, answered that the children were not al dead, but [only] that the Oke or Divell did sucke the blood from their left breast [of those], who chanced to be his by lot, till they were dead. But the rest were kept in the wildernesse by the yong men till nine moneths were expired, during which time they must not converse with any: and of these, were made their priests and conjurers." The werowance continued by saying that the sacrifice was considered to be so necessary, that if it were omitted, "their Oke or divel" and all the other gods, would not let the people have "deare, turkies, corne, nor fish: and yet besides, hee would make great slaughter amongst them."

Beverley thinks the sacrifice of children, described by Smith and Strachey, was the Huskanaw, as he calls it, or a hardening ceremony with which he was familiar in the latter part of the century. It was practiced only once every fourteen or sixteen years, or when the young men happened to grow up. Beverley does not associate it with the priesthood, but declares that it was a form of discipline and testing to determine which of the youths would make worthy candidates for admission to the ranks of great men, or counselors of the nation.

The young men to be huskanawed were kept in an enclosure in the woods for several months, and were given a concoction made from roots which drove them "stark staring mad." They were kept in this "raving condition" for eighteen or twenty days, after which the intoxicating diet was gradually reduced. But they were brought to the village while they were "still wild and crazy." As a result of this huskanawing, the young men were supposed to forget, or pretend to forget, everything in their past—their wealth, parents, tongue, etc., and learn "All things perfectly over again. Thus they unlive their former lives, and commence men, by forgetting that they ever have been boys." If they indicated they remembered their past, they would be huskanawed again. No doubt, if they did remember, they made every effort to conceal it. Beverley also adds that occasionally a young man did not survive the experience.

The Virginia Siouans of the seventeenth century no doubt practiced huskanawing because Lawson finds it among the North Carolina Siouans of the early part of the eighteenth century. His description of the ceremony is very much like that of Beverley, with the exception that both boys and girls were subjected to it among the Siouans. Its purpose was to make the young people obey and respect "their superiors." In addition, Lawson says that it was supposed to "Harden them ever after to the fatigue of war,

64

hunting, and all manner of hardship, which their way of living exposes them to. Beside, they [the Indians] add, that it carries off those infirm weak bodies, that would have been only a burden and disgrace to their nation."

MEDICAL TREATMENTS

The priests were the doctors among the Virginia Algonquians. Sacred formulae, rituals and medical practices were closely associated. Spelman and Smith speak of the charms, rattles, infernal words, and actions that were an important part of every treatment.

Spelman gives us the best picture of a priest-doctor in action, and of his psychological treatment perhaps which preceded the physical: "When any be sicke among them, ther preests cums unto the partye whom he layeth on the ground uppon a matt, and having a boule of water, sett betwene him and the sicke partye; and a rattle by it, the priest kneelinge by the sick mans side dipps his hand in the boule, which takinge up full of watter, he supps into his mouth, spowting it out againe, uppon his oune armes, and brest, then takes he the rattle, and with one hand takes that, and with the other he beates his brest, makinge a great noyes, which havinge dunn he easilye riseth (as loith to wake the sicke bodye), first with one legge, then with the other, And beinge now gott up, he leaysuerly goeth about the sicke man shakinge his rattle very [easily] softly over his bodye: and with his hand he stroketh the greaved parts of the sicke, then doth he besprinkell him with water mumblinge certayne words over him, and so for that time leave him."

The priests had acquired and passed on through the years some general medical knowledge. They knew that a wound should heal from the bottom, and if it became infected they would cut into it and drain off the impurities by suction. Then they would apply powder made from certain crushed roots or juice made from certain herbs. Deep wounds or compound fractures were mostly beyond their ability to cure. Several rather violent laxatives were known by them and used every spring. For dropsy, swelling, and aches, they prepared a small oven-shaped sweat-lodge covered with mats placed together so closely, that it was possible to heat the interior with a few hot coals covered with a pot. After the sweat-lodge had become very warm, the patient was made to sit inside and perspire extremely. For swelling the priests also used small cone-shaped splinters of touchwood which they stuck in the swollen part and burned close to the flesh, and "From thence," says Smith, "draw the corruption with their mouths."

Reeds were used for cauterizing, and inflammation of the skin was relieved by scarifying or scratching the epidermis with a rattle-snake's tooth.

Their remedies or medicines, for the most part, were made of roots, and of bark of trees; leaves of either herbs or trees were used to a much lesser extent, according to Beverley. He also adds that "What they give inwardly, they infuse with water, and what they apply outwardly, they stamp or bruise, adding water to it."

In Beverley's time, the sweat-lodge was also very popular. It was used by the Indians to refresh their tired bodies, and to relieve "Agues, aches, or pains in their limbs." At this date, the lodge was no longer built of mats, but was "Made like an oven in some bank near the water side." It held six or eight Indians at a time and was heated with red hot stones, on which water was poured at intervals to raise a steam. Now and then the priest would pour water on those taking the treatment to keep them from fainting. After they had perspired freely and stayed in the lodge as long as they could, they would rush out and plunge into the river. The cold water, they believed, closed their pores and preserved them from catching cold. Subsequent to the bath, the Indians would rub on their bodies a yellow ointment which was made of puccoon (bloodroot) and a sort of wild angelica, mixed with bear fat. This ointment was highly prized because it not only closed the pores, kept the skin soft, and made the

66

Indians "nimble and active," but it completely discouraged "Lice, fleas and other troublesome vermine."

We have no account of the medical practices among the Virginia Siouans of the seventeenth century. Lawson's history, though later, suggests that they did not differ greatly from those of the Virginia Algonquian.

Various Means of Communication

The Virginia Indians used various methods for conveying thought to each other and to strangers. Language, of course, was the principal medium, and since there was very little difference in the tongue of the Virginia Algonquians, all the Tidewater tribes had no difficulty conversing with each other. However, it was an entirely different story when Tidewater natives met Indians from another nation. The language barrier was present. According to Smith the Siouan nations, as well as other nations adjoining Powhatan's territory, spoke "Sundry languages" and "al those not any one understandeth another but by interpreters." It would seem probable, therefore, that in every large tribe there were a few men with language ability who mastered one or more foreign tongues and who acted as interpreters when the occasion arose. An example of this is found in the story of Smith's exploration of the Rappahannock River in July 1608. When the English had gone some distance up the river, they captured a Hassininga Indian of the Piedmont section, and Mosco, a Powhatan Indian of Wighcocomoco, who accompanied the English, had to act as interpreter.

Beverley tells us that in the seventeenth century the Occaneechi tongue became a sort of general language for all the tribes which traded with that small but wealthy nation. The Occaneechi, as we have previously stated, belonged to the eastern Siouan group. They had their home on an island in the Roanoke River, near the present Clarksville, Virginia. It is easy to

67

believe that their importance in the Indian trade world would lead to the development of a trade jargon based on their language.

A reference is made by Percy to the probable use of smoke signaling by the Chesapeake Indians. But Percy was not sure that the fire was made for that specific purpose, and since this practice is not mentioned by the other early writers, one cannot be too assertive in claiming that smoke signaling was used by the Virginia Algonquians as a means of communicating.

When the Tidewater Indians traveled beyond their territory, they painted tribal marks upon their shoulders for identification purposes. These marks, according to Beverley, usually represented one or more arrows and their arrangement clearly indicated the tribes to which the individuals belonged.

The English soon learned that there were various signs which were used by the Indians to convey meanings. For example, to indicate peaceful intentions, the Indians would lay down their arms. Distrust, and anger were apparent if the Indians fixed an arrow to the bow and held it in readiness, or if they shook their tomahawks and clubs over their heads, or if they made bold speech. Solemn promises were bound or oaths taken by pointing to the sun and clapping the right hand upon the heart. Several signs of friendship and welcome were used, such as, spreading mats for the visitors to sit upon, distributing tobacco, offering a pipe to smoke, embracing, exchanging of parts of clothing, presentation of gifts, striking head and breast and then those of visitor to indicate brotherhood, and shouting one or more times when a short way off as a greeting, and also when leave-taking. Pantomime and signs easily suggested hunger, sleep, fatigue, joy, anger, etc. Imitation of the walk, body motions, and manner of animals, at which the Indians were notably adept, conveyed the information to the visitor almost as well as it could have been done by word.

Making simple enumerations without the aid of language presented no great problem. In Archer's *Relation* of the discovery of the James in June 1607, we find an interesting account of the simple method the English used to dispose of such a difficulty: "There was an olde man with King Pamaunche who wee understood to be 110 yere olde; for Nauiraus with being with us in our boate had learned me so much of the languadg[e], and was so excellently ingenious in signing out his meaning, that I could make him understand me, and perceive him also wellny in any thing. But this knowledg[e] our Captaine gatt by taking a bough and singling of the leaves, let one drop after another, saying *caische* which is 10 so first Nauiraus tooke 11 beanes and tolde them to us, pointing to this olde fellow, then 110 beanes; by which he awnswered to our demaund for 10 yeares a beane, and also every yeare by it selfe."

Seasons and Festivals

The Powhatan Indians had an annual economic cycle of five seasons. Smith tells us that their winter was called *Popanow,* the spring *Cattapeuk,* the summer *Cohattayough,* the earing of their corn *Nepinough,* the harvest and fall of the leaf *Taquitock.*

A hundred years later, Beverley enlarges the subject: "They make their account by units, tens, hundreds, etc., as we do; but they reckon the years by the winters, or *Cohonks,* as they call them; which is a name taken from the note of the wild geese, intimating so many times of the wild geese coming to them, which is every winter. They distinguish the several parts of the year, by five seasons, *viz.* The budding or blossoming of the spring; the earing of the corn, or roasting ear time; the summer, or highest sun; the corn-gathering, or fall of the leaf; and the winter, or *Cohonks.* They count the months likewise by the moons, tho not with any relation to so many in a year, as we do: but they make them return again by the same name, as the moon of stags, the corn moon, the first and second moon of *Cohonks,* etc. They have no distinction of the hours of the day, but divide it only into three parts, the rise, power, and lowering of the sun. And

69

they keep their account by knots on a string, or notches on a stick, not unlike the *Peruvian quippoes*."

September to November was usually the time of plenty. The Indians could enjoy the harvest of their fields and gardens, as well as large supplies of fish and animal food. Smith says that during this period of the year they had their chief feasts, and sacrifices. And Beverley states that they had feasts for certain seasons. "They solemnize a day for the plentiful coming of their wild fowl, such as geese, ducks, teal, etc., for the return of their hunting seasons, and for the ripening of certain fruits: but the greatest annual feast they have is at the time of their corn-gathering, at which they revel several days together. To these they universally contribute, as they do to the gathering in the corn. On this occasion they have their greatest variety of pastimes, and more especially of their war-dances, and heroick songs: in which they boast, that their corn being now gather'd, they have store enough for their women and children; and have nothing to do, but to go to war, travel, and to seek out for new adventures."

Lawson's observations of the North Carolina Siouans would lead us to believe that the Virginia Siouans of the seventeenth century had almost the same activities in the several seasons as the Virginia Algonquians.

TRADE

We know that prior to 1607 trade among the Virginia Indians was rather extensive, but it was apparently not so intensive. Reports of trade with far off tribes were made by the Powhatan Indians to the early settlers. Archaeological evidence found on village sites and in burial pits of the late prehistoric period indicate a limited amount of trade which consisted of copper, marine shells, shell beads, a few objects of bone and an occasional soapstone pipe. There was probably some traffic in perishable objects, such as, mats, furs, grain, tobacco, wooden utensils, etc.

Barter in stone materials for making implements was inconsiderable.

Shells and shell beads of Atlantic coast origin have been found in many parts of the state. Beads of conch shell, of Atlantic Ocean origin as well as of the Gulf of Mexico, have been recovered from several sites. Shells and shell beads served as a medium of exchange and indicate trade from the coast inland.

The colonists found that the Tidewater Indians placed great value on copper, and they reported that it came from a great distance inland. It is now believed that some of it was of Virginia origin, but that the greater part of it found its way to the coast from the Lake Superior region. Pre-contact sites have also yielded copper.

There is evidence, therefore, of the establishment of some trade in Virginia before the coming of the whites. In order to go from the coast inland and vice versa to engage in trade or to travel within or outside the tribal regions, for friendly or unfriendly reasons, the Indians traveled the same paths year after year. Animals had originally made most of these paths, and later when the Indians came, they continued to be used jointly by man and beast. Due to the habit of the animals and Indians of marching in single file, the paths or trails were usually not over twenty inches wide. The Indians more frequently selected those that led along high ground or low ridges where there would be less underbrush, and fewer deep streams to cross. Those that ran through the gaps rather than over the high points were chosen in the mountainous sections.

The first white explorers and traders in Virginia found these trails and used them. Later these paths determined the wagon roads and in some cases even the settlements.

A few of the major trails that played important roles in the early history of Virginia might be considered briefly at this point in our story. William E. Myer's splendid study entitled *Indian*

71

Trails of the Southeast, published in the *Forty-Second Annual Report* of the Bureau of American Ethnology is our source of information.

There was the well-known Occaneechi Path which led from Bermuda Hundred on the James River and Fort Henry, at the present Petersburg, Virginia, in a southwestern direction to the trading town of the Occaneechi Indians, at the present Clarksville, Virginia. From there it went on through southwestern North Carolina, northwestern South Carolina to the site of the present Augusta, Georgia. This trail did not assume great importance until after the coming of the whites. Then it assumed great prominence as a route for traders and settlers, and in time it developed into a turnpike and finally into the roadbed of the Southern Railway.

The Petersburg-Saponi Trail ran from the present site of Petersburg probably by way of Farmville to Saponi town on Otter Creek, Campbell County, Virginia.

The Pamunkey and New Rivers Trail ran from the Pamunkey River to Charlottesville, to Staunton, turned in a southwestern direction probably via Clifton Forge and Covington into West Virginia where it met the New and Kanawha rivers and followed them to the Ohio.

One of the most famous trails which ran through Virginia was the Chesapeake Branch of the Great Indian Warpath. The trail entered Virginia about three miles west of Bristol, split for a short distance and joined at Wyndale, and thence via Abingdon to Marion, and across the New River near Radford. From that point it led to Salem, Roanoke, Lexington, Staunton, Winchester, and into Maryland and Pennsylvania and states farther north.

The Ohio Branch of the Great Indian Warpath led from the southwestern part of the state up the Holston Valley to Saltville, Virginia, to New River, and down the New and Kanawha rivers to eastern Ohio and western Pennsylvania.

The Great Indian War Path and its branches were important

trading and war paths. They later served the white settlers who moved into Virginia from the north and opened all the valley section of Virginia, and spread through the southwestern part into Kentucky, Tennessee, and West Virginia.

During the first four decades of the century, the Virginia trade turned to the north along the Chesapeake Bay region, and the waterways served as means of travel and transportation. When the trade shifted to the south and southwest, the trails assumed great importance.

Very soon after the settlement was made at Jamestown, Captain John Smith recognized the need for organizing trade with the Indians, and in order to do that, he visited as soon as possible the tribes settled along the main rivers of the Tidewater section. Smith was interested in foods, especially corn, that could keep the colonists alive.

Corn, obtained by trade or the use of force, saved the life of the colony on more than one occasion. But, after 1614, we find that the colonists were growing their own supply of corn, except for a few years when the feverish interest in growing tobacco dangerously reduced the corn crop. From that date on, the Indians were frequently forced to buy corn from the English with skins or by mortgaging their lands. Furthermore, the English were becoming more interested in obtaining skins than the necessities.

Almost from the beginning the English found it necessary to pass regulations relative to trade. As soon as the demand for skins made itself felt, there were colonists who were willing to provide the Indians with guns and ammunition in order to accelerate the killing of fur bearing animals, and thereby increase their own profits. Consequently, as early as 1617 commissioners were appointed to trade with the northern part of Virginia which provided most of the trade at that time. By 1624 special license to trade had to be obtained from the Governor. Long before the massacre of 1622 laws were passed which provided the death penalty for making guns and ammunition available to the Indians. These laws, with some changes in penalties—providing either death, or life imprisonment and forfeiture of wealth—were re-enacted during the second and third quarter of the century.

Trade with the Indians fluctuated, of course, during the century depending largely upon their relations, friendly or unfriendly with the English, and upon favorable or unfavorable laws. After the wars of 1622, 1644, and 1675, there was some interruption of trade but not as much as might be expected.

Only beaver and otter skins were in demand in the early years, but in 1620 the Virginia Company of London enlarged the list of furs by adding lucern, marten, wildcat, fox, and muskrat with high prices offered.

The first real organization of the Indian trade, especially on the part of private parties, was made by William Claiborne. Sir George Yeardley, as Governor of Virginia, gave Claiborne his commission to trade with the Indians in 1627, and about three years later he set up a storehouse at Hampton as a supply base for Kent Island from which he carried on his trade up the Chesapeake Bay. He developed a very brisk trade, the success of which depended largely upon an abundant supply of truck to barter with the Indians. From various sources we learn that this truck consisted chiefly of glass beads, copper rings, iron and copper bracelets, copper belts, copper kettles, trade pipes, trading cloth, matchcoats, pins, needles, nails, looking-glasses, corn, iron wire, small knives, small hatchets, scissors, wooden combs, fish-hooks, toys, and as Smith expresses it, "such like trash." In return for this truck the traders usually wanted furs, occasionally canoes, game, wooden platters, pottery, baskets, rush mats, etc.

Another chief promoter of Virginia Indian trade to the northward in the early years was Henry Fleet. He had been sent with Captain Henry Spelman in 1623 to trade for corn with the Anocostans up the Potomac. Spelman and eighteen of his men

74

were killed by these Indians and Henry Fleet and the others were held captive. It was not until 1627 that Fleet's friends finally contrived to ransom him. Thus, his four years of captivity had given him the opportunity to acquire much knowledge of the Indians which he could profitably use as a trader. Both Fleet and Claiborne were backed financially by London merchants interested in promoting a Chesapeake Indian trade.

After 1644 a stronger effort was made by the government to organize the Indian trade. The construction of four forts was ordered by provisions of statutes of 1645 and 1646—Fort Royal (alias Rickahack) at Pamunkey, Fort Charles at the falls of the James, Fort James on the Ridge of the Chickahominy, and Fort Henry at the falls of the Appomattox. These forts were established primarily for protection but soon became trading centers, and the Indians had to trade there. Captain Abraham Wood, in charge of Fort Henry, was soon doing a thriving business because the heavy trading was already shifting from north to south. This shift in the trading was furthered to a great extent by the encouragement that Governor William Berkeley gave to explorations to the south and west.

In order to provide the Indians with greater access to the necessities of life and make their commodities easily available to the whites an act was passed in 1656 which provided that the Indians must have tickets obtained from some person nominated on the head of each river where the Indians lived. With these tickets the Indians could enter fenced plantations in amity without arms to fowl, fish, or gather wild fruits.

In April 1658 the Assembly passed an act which encouraged miscellaneous trade to the detriment of professional traders and revealed a complete change of attitude toward barter and trade of guns, powder, and shot. The Assembly, recognizing that the neighboring "Plantations both English and forrainers" were furnishing the Indians with all the guns and ammunition they could purchase and were receiving most of the beaver trade, enacted that "Every man may freely trade for gunns, powder and shott."

However, the fur trade was henceforth to be strictly governed by the Governor and the Assembly. In 1660 a law was enacted which provided that no person should trade with the Indians for any beaver, otter or any furs unless he first obtained a commission from the Governor.

An important act which reveals the relationship between the whites and the Indians was passed in March 1661. This act provided that the bounds between the English and the Indians were to be fixed by commissioners and viewed annually. In order to provide free communication and distinguish between Indian nations, silver, or copper badges, with the name of the town engraved thereon, were given to all the chiefs of the neighboring tribes under Virginia's protection. No Indian was to enter the English bounds without a badge, and if an Indian were found in the bounds without a badge, he would be kept in custody until his king or great man ransomed him "By paying one hundred armed length of rohonoake" to be disposed of by the public.

An Act of 1665 prohibited the sale of arms and ammunition to the Indians and discontinued this loose policy of trade. Now that the English had driven out the Dutch, who had been trading arms with the Indians and getting most of the trade, there was no longer any need for this dangerous policy of permitting "Every man" to trade freely "for gunns, powder and shott." This act was re-enacted in 1675.

After 1670 efforts were concentrated more and more on explorations to the south and west, promoted especially by General Abraham Wood and Captain William Byrd.

By 1677 the Grand Assembly passed an act permitting free trade with the friendly Indians. The Act also gave the Indians the right to bring any commodities to the several marts or fairs designated for various sections of the Tidewater to be held at different times of the year. The Indians had to come unarmed.

In 1680 the Assembly passed an Act providing "Free and open trade for all persons at all times and places with our friendly Indians." This policy was to prevail in the future.

In 1691 the General Assembly passed an Act repealing all former laws restraining trade with the Indians and provided that henceforth "There be a free and open trade for all persons at all times and at all places with all Indians whatsoever." This Act was re-enacted in the revisal in 1705 and again in the edition of 1733.

Loss of Population, Wars, and Displacement

James Mooney estimates (1928) that the population of the Powhatans was about 9,000 at the beginning of the seventeenth century. Smith allows them 2,385 fighting men, but he omits in his enumeration several tribal capitals which would bring the total to about 2,500. Strachey, thinking in terms of about 1612, estimates 3,320 fighting men, but this figure is considered too high by Mooney who uses Smith's estimation.

The census of the Powhatans taken in 1669 shows only 528 warriors which indicates a population of approximately 2,000. The Eastern Shore population is not noted.

In his *History of Virginia*, 1705, Beverley says that the Indians of Virginia all together could not raise 500 fighting men. If we subtract from that number the 100 Nottoway and the 30 Meherrin which he includes in the total, that leaves less than 370 Powhatans including those on the Eastern Shore, or a population of men, women, and children of about 1,200.

Estimation of the population of the Siouan and of the Iroquoian tribes in the state during the century is largely guesswork. They have been given a total of 8,000 to 9,000 for the year 1600. The Siouans numbered perhaps 6,300 and the Iroquoians about 2,600. By the middle of the century each group numbered probably less than 1,200 souls.

The next report we have on the population of the Siouans is that of Governor Spotswood in 1715, in which he states that the Indians of Fort Christanna, including the Tutelo, Saponi, Occaneechi, and Manahoac numbered 300.

Population figures are available on two of the Iroquoian groups. The Meherrin group began the century with about 700 souls. In the 1669 census they had approximately 180, and by the end of the century slightly over 100. The Nottoway in 1600 had about 1,500. Beverley estimates in 1705 that they had about 330 souls. The Cherokee Indian population probably fluctuated greatly during the seventeenth century. It is doubtful if their population in Virginia ever exceeded 800.

Thus within one hundred years the population of the powerful Powhatan Confederacy had decreased in strength from about 9,000 souls to 1,200. The entire Indian population in Virginia had declined from about 18,000 to 2,000.

This calamitous loss of population among the Indians was brought about by wars with the English, wars with enemy tribes, smallpox and other diseases, and a general disorganization of their society.

In spite of the fact that the English had been enjoined by the Virginia council to be just, kind, and charitable to the Indians, these instructions were difficult to follow. By 1608 the English had to resort to force to obtain corn and other foods when the Indians refused to trade. The Indians soon realized that the English could take what they wanted. Several harsh proofs of this fact followed, such as: their attack on the Nansemond in 1608, the killing of a number of Paspahegh in 1610, the destruction of Kecoughtan in 1610, and of Appomattoc in the following year.

Powhatan entertained hopes for awhile perhaps that the English had no intention of remaining in his country, and Smith, during his captivity at Werowocomoco in January 1608, was careful to aver that such was the case. It is doubtful if Powhatan took this statement very seriously. At any rate, the record seems

"Their dances which they use at their high feasts." John White Drawing.
Photograph by The Smithsonian Institution.

"Theire sitting at meate." By John White. Photograph by The Smithsonian Institution.

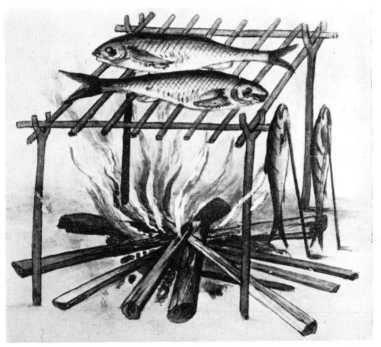

"The broyling of their fish over the flame of fier." By John White.
Photograph by The Smithsonian Institution.

Ears of corn boiling in Indian earthenware stew pot (corn on the cob). By John White. Photograph by The Smithsonian Institution.

to make it clear that Powhatan and Opechancanough, as early as the spring of 1608, began to plot the destruction of the English. But the Indians' awe and fear of guns and cannon, and coats of mail made early concerted action on their part very difficult. The marriage of Pocahontas to John Rolfe in April, 1614, postponed any idea of an all out effort to destroy the English.

Powhatan died in April 1618, and was succeeded in chief power by his lame brother Opitchapan. Within a short time he retired in favor of Opechancanough. The way was now open for the bitter, aggressive, and implacable enemy of the English to prepare a massive and if possible fatal blow against them. It did not fall until March 22, 1622. But it was so unexpected and effective that within a few hours 347 (some accounts estimate as high as 400) colonists had been killed.

The massacre aroused in the colonists a burning desire for revenge, and they knew that their superior organization and weapons would make it possible for them to gratify it to the utmost. Gone now was the hope to establish a university at Henrico and christianize and train in useful employment the Indian children. Such a hope was in the first place idealistic and premature. Years of peace had made the English lose sight of the reality of the situation. The civilization of the white men had little attraction for the Indians, and they were by no means ready to accept it. They felt no urge to change their religion, which gave them joy and satisfaction, for another. They could feel nothing but bitterness for the intruders who were taking away their lands and threatening their way of life.

After the massacre the Virginia Company of London and the colonists felt that it was futile to try to convert the Indians to the Christian religion or to the European economy. The only solution was to exterminate them. Instructions came to wage any kind of war, to kill the men and women, and capture the young people who could be used for profitable labor. The nimble Indians were hard to catch, but the colonists had a very effective method of retaliation. They burned the Indian villages, destroyed their crops, weirs, and canoes. During every summer for the next decade, raiding parties were sent out to harvest or destroy crops as fast as they were made. Forces were sent against the large villages along all the major rivers, and thousands of bushels of corn were taken or destroyed. Hundreds of Indians were killed either by bullets or starvation as a result of this determined and relentless effort to root them out.

Twenty-two years later, in spite of the great decrease in the population of the Indians, and increase in the English population, 8,000, as compared with about 1,300 in 1624, Opechancanough, now infirm but still full of hatred for the intruders, made a last desperate attempt. As before, the attack was carefully planned and came as a surprise to the colonists on April 17, 1644. During the two days of the attack, from 300 to 500 colonists were killed.

Retaliation on the part of the colonists was swift and severe. Two principal expeditions were prepared. One was sent against the Pamunkey and the other against the Chickahominy. The method of burning the towns and destroying the crops was again adopted. The war went on until October 1646, or about two and one-half years. During that time Opechancanough was captured and killed, and the various tribes so completely subdued and broken that the colony's Assembly reported in 1646 that the Indians were "So routed and dispersed that they are no longer a nation, and we now suffer only from robbery by a few starved outlaws."

A treaty was made with Necotowance, the successor to Opechancanough, because it "Would conduce to the better being and comoditie of the country," and it was confirmed by the Assembly in 1646. By its terms the Indians agreed to abandon all the land between the York and the James from the falls downward, and their territory was restricted to the land north of the York. They acknowledged the overlordship of the English king, and bound themselves to pay tribute of "Twenty beaver skins att the goeing away of geese yearely." One of the most significant features of this treaty was the recognition of the Indians' need and enjoyment of their own lands.

A specific record of trouble with the Rappahannock Indians is found in 1654. In that year the Grand Assembly ordered a defensive march of one hundred and seventy men against the Rappahannock. No record exists which relates the outcome of this affair. Apparently a satisfactory settlement was made without recourse to arms.

In 1655 or 1656, six or seven hundred Richahecrians, as the Virginians called them, (probably Manahoac and Tutelo tribes) moved down from the mountains and settled near Richmond. Their enemies, the Susquehanna, had probably forced them out of their homeland. The colonists did not want such a large number of unwelcomed visitors so close to their settlement, and it was determined that they should be driven out. Approximately 100 militia-men under Colonel Edward Hill, assisted by Totopotomoi, chief of the Pamunkey, with 100 men, were sent against them. The colonists suffered a severe defeat, and Totopotomoi and nearly all his braves were killed.

In 1675 and 1676, raids on Virginia's frontier settlement by the Susquehanna (Conestoga) and Doeg Indians of Maryland, and by the Occaneechi and other tribes of southwestern Virginia, caused great concern among the prominent planters. Eventually, Nathaniel Bacon, a planter and owner of two plantations, led unauthorized expeditions against the Indians. About the end of April 1676, he first marched against the Susquehanna, who in their bloody retreat across the state from the Potomac River to the Occaneechi village on an island in the Roanoke River, had murdered Bacon's overseer at Bacon's Quarter, at the present site of Richmond.

The accounts of what happened at Occaneechi differ somewhat. Apparently Bacon made friends with the Occaneechi and

81

persuaded them to fall upon the Susquehanna. The result was a bloody battle in which thirty Susquehanna warriors, and all their women and children were killed. Then when the Occaneechi refused to provide promised food, Bacon and his men fell upon them and killed about 100 men, two chiefs, and many women and children.

Soon after this disastrous defeat, the remaining members of the Occaneechi tribe left their lands on the Roanoke and settled on the Eno River in North Carolina where they were visited by Lawson in 1701.

In the latter part of the summer of 1676 Bacon, now with a commission which he had demanded and obtained, led his men against the Pamunkey Indians because he was convinced that they were responsible for the recent raids along the York River. After slaying a few Indians of both sexes in several minor engagements, Bacon's forces finally came upon the main settlement of the Pamunkey in Dragon Swamp. As the English charged, the Indians fled, but not before some were killed and forty-five were captured. All their goods, consisting of mats, baskets, skins, furs, matchcoats, cloth and other trade goods, and wampum and Roanoke (their money) fell into the hands of the English.

A general treaty of peace was concluded on May 29, 1677 at Middle Plantation, the present site of Williamsburg, with all the tribes in relation to the Virginia government. Ten tribes, which now declared their subjection to the Queen of Pamunkey, signed the treaty: the Pamunkey, Appomattoc, Weanoc, Nansemond, Nantaughtacund, Portabaccos, that is, all of the old Powhatan Confederacy, and the Nottoway, Meherrin, Monocan, and Saponi. By terms of the treaty, the Indians acknowledged dependency upon the king of England. They were bound to give notice of the appearance of any strange Indians on the frontier, and were to assist the English against the enemy if requested. The possession of their tribal lands was confirmed, and those tribes with insufficient land were to be given more, subject each to an annual quitrent of three arrows and twenty beaver skins to be brought in the month of March every year to the Governor's residence.

Trouble with raiding parties of northern Indians on the frontiers arose from time to time during the remainder of the century, but this treaty of 1677 is considered by some students of history to mark the end of the Indian period in Virginia.

The other Indian groups in the state were not brought as closely in contact with the English as the Powhatan group, and consequently had fewer clashes and lost fewer lives.

There is no record of any serious conflict between the colonists and the Iroquoian groups—the Cherokee, Nottoway, and the Meherrin.

Several of the Siouan groups were involved in wars with the colonists and suffered losses. The Manahoac, and the Nahyssan (Monahassanugh) were probably among those tribes which settled near Richmond in 1655 or 1656 and defeated Colonel Hill and his Pamunkey allies. The victorious Indian groups evidently lost some fighting men. Several years prior to 1676 the Nahyssan, Tutelo, and Saponi, the latter two tribes probably remnants of the Manahoac and Monacan, had moved to islands in the Roanoke River in the Occaneechi country, and were also the unfortunate victims of Bacon's anger.

The greatest loss suffered by these people in warfare was, no doubt, at the hands of roving bands of Iroquois and Susquehanna who were their implacable enemies. The movement southward of some of the Siouan tribes began soon after the middle of the century. Others moved perhaps two decades later, but in each case the reason was to escape the attacks of the northern Indians.

Another enemy in the form of disease introduced by the whites greatly reduced the Virginia Indian population during the seventeenth century. No accurate information is available on the number of Indians carried away by disease, yet it is a known fact that they lacked immunity to smallpox, tuberculosis, and other old world ills which were brought in early.

In the early narrative of Walter Russell and Anas Todkill, relating to the visit made by Smith to the Werowance of Accomac in June 1608, there is an apparent reference to smallpox. The werowance told Smith and his companions that two children had recently died, and that a great part of his people went to view the bodies because "They reflected to the eies of the beholders such pleasant delightful countenances, as though they had regained their vital spirits. This as a miracle, drew many to behold them: all which, not long after died, and not any one escaped." Venereal diseases brought great suffering and death to many of the natives. It has already been pointed out that evidence of syphilis has been found in the skeletal remains recovered from some of the early contact sites. In 1617, during Argall's administration, there was a general sickness among the whites and Indians which was apparently quite a death-dealing epidemic among both people. The various imported diseases probably spread quickly to the Siouan and Iroquoian groups in the state and were just as devastating to them as they were to the Powhatans.

The introduction of rum by a few unscrupulous traders to the Virginia Indians proved to be a great evil. Prior to the coming of the whites, the Indians had no distilled liquor. But as soon as they made the acquaintance of rum, they developed a craze for it and were ready to drink on any and all occasions when it was obtainable. This new passion no doubt helped to debase them and demoralize their society. The colonists and most of the traders recognized the danger, and consequently laws were passed by the colony of Virginia to regulate the sale of rum to the Indians, but these laws were as difficult to enforce as those prohibiting the sale of guns and ammunition.

Beverley gives us the best description of the weakness of the Virginia Indians for strong drink: "For their strong drink, they

84

are altogether beholding to us, and are so greedy of it, that most of them will be drunk as often as they find an opportunity: notwithstanding which, it is a prevailing humour among them, not to taste any strong drink at all, unless they can get enough to make them quite drunk, and then they go as solemnly about it, as if it were part of their religion."

Such is the broadly sketched picture of the Virginia Indians of the seventeenth century—a century which was probably the most tragic period in their long existence. The several groups in Virginia had reached the highest point in the gradual development of their civilization. They enjoyed their lands, customs, and religion. Their economic system operated well. But when pitted against the culture of the English, the civilization of the Indians was powerless. It proved to be impossible for two cultures so fundamentally different to exist side by side. The feeble and belated efforts to find the answer to the situation came to naught. Wars, imported disease, liquor, and general moral destruction did their work so well that the Virginia tribes which were numerous, strong, and dominant in 1600 had disappeared or had almost completely disintegrated by 1700.

BIBLIOGRAPHY

Archaeological Society of Virginia. Quarterly Bulletin, vols. 1-10. (These bulletins contain many excellent articles on Virginia archaeology.)

Beverley, Robert. *The History and Present State of Virginia.* Published for The Institute of Early American History and Culture. Edited by Louis B. Wright. Chapel Hill, 1947. (This book, first published in 1705, has Part III devoted to Indian life and customs during the seventeenth century.)

Brown, Alexander. *The Genesis of the United States.* New York, 1890. 2 vols.

Bushnell, David I. Jr., *Virginia—From Early Sources, American Anthropologist,* 9 (1907), 45-56.

—. *Virginia Before Jamestown. Smithsonian Miscellaneous Collections,* 100 (1940), 125-158.

—. *Indian Sites Below the Falls of the Rappahannock. Smithsonian Miscellaneous Collections,* 96 (1937), 1-65.

—. *The Five Monacan Towns in Virginia, 1607. Smithsonian Miscellaneous Collections,* 82 (1930), 1-38.

—. *The Manahoac Tribes in Virginia, 1608. Smithsonian Miscellaneous Collections,* 94 (1935), 1-56.

—. *Tribal Migrations East of the Mississippi. Smithsonian Miscellaneous Collections,* 89 (1934), 1-9.

Craven, Wesley Frank, *Indian Policy in Early Virginia. William and Mary Quarterly,* 3rd Series, 1 (1944), 65-82.

Claiborne, John Herbert. *William Claiborne of Virginia. With Some Account of his Pedigree.* New York, 1917.

Evans, Clifford. *A Ceramic Study of Virginia Archeology. Bureau of American Ethnology,* 160 (1955), 1-164.

Force, Peter. *Tracts and other papers, relating principally to the origin, settlement, and progress of the colonies in North America, from the year of discovery of the country to the year 1776.* Washington, 1836-46. 4 vols. (Reprinted under auspices of the Out-of-Print Book Committee of the American Library Association, New York, Peter Smith, 1947.)

Griffin, James B. *Archeology of Eastern United States,* The University of Chicago Press, 1952.

Hariot, Thomas. *Narrative of the first English Plantation of Virginia.* London, B. Quaritch. Reprint. 1893. (Although this account is concerned with the Algonquian Indians of North Carolina, it is an im-

86

portant source of information for the student of the Algonquian Indians of Virginia because of the similarity of the two groups.)

Hening, William W. *The Statutes at Large; being a collection of all the laws of Virginia.* Richmond, 1809-1823. 13 vols.

Hodge, Frederick W. *Handbook of American Indians North of Mexico. Bureau of American Ethnology,* 30 (1907-1910). (An encyclopedia of Indian tribes and Indian customs.)

Lawson, John. *History of North Carolina, containing the exact description and natural history of that country.* Richmond, 1937. (The first edition of this work appeared in London in 1709. Other editions followed in 1714 and 1718. Lawson's account of the manners and customs of the Indian tribes is the best of that period.)

Lederer, John. *The Discoveries of John Lederer, in three several Marches from Virginia to the West of Carolina, and other parts of the Continent: Begun in March 1669, and ended in September 1670. Together with a General Map of the Whole Territory which he traversed. Collected and Translated out of Latine from his Discourse and Writings, by Sir William Talbot, Baronet.* London, 1672. Reprinted for George P. Humphrey, Rochester, New York, 1902.

Lorant, Stephan. *The New World, the first Pictures of America made by John White and Jacques Le Moyne and engraved by Theodore De Bry, with contemporary narratives of the Huguenot Settlement in Florida 1562-1563, and the Virginia Colony 1585-1590.* New York, 1946. (White's drawings of the native inhabitants of the Carolina coast provide an invaluable source of information for the student of the southern Algonquian Indians.)

Michel, Francis Louis. *Report of the journey of Francis Louis Michel from Berne, Switzerland, to Virginia, October 2, 1701-December 1, 1702. Virginia Magazine of History and Biography,* 24 (1916), 1-43, 113-141, 275-303. Translated and edited by William J. Hinke.

Mook, Maurice. *The Anthropological Position of the Indian Tribes of Tidewater Virginia, William and Mary College Quarterly,* 2nd Series, 23 (1943), 27-40.

—. *Virginia Ethnology from an early Relation. William and Mary College Quarterly,* 2nd Series, 23 (1943), 101-129.

—. *The Ethnological Significance of Tindall's Map of Virginia, 1608, William and Mary College Quarterly,* 2nd Series, 23 (1943), 372-408.

—. *The Aboriginal Population of Tidewater Virginia. American Anthropologist,* 40, (1944), 193-208.

Mooney, James. *The Aboriginal Population of America North of Mexico. Smithsonian Miscellaneous Collections,* 80 (1928), 1-40.

—. *The Powhatan Confederacy, Past and Present. American Anthropologist,* 9 (1907), 129-152.

—. *Siouan Tribes of the East. Bureau of American Ethnology,* Bulletin 22 (1895).

Morrison, A. J. *The Virginia Indian Trade to 1673. William and Mary College Quarterly,* 2nd Series, 1 (1921), 217-236.

Myer, William E. *Indian Trails of the Southeast. Bureau of American Ethnology,* 42nd Annual Report, 1924-1925, (1928), 727-857.

Rights, Douglas L. *The American Indian in North Carolina,* Durham, 1947.

Smith, John. *Travels and Works.* Ed. by Edward Arber. New edition with introduction by A. G. Bradley. Edinburgh, 1910. 2 vols. (Smith's map of Virginia, drawn in 1608 and published in 1612, is amazingly complete and accurate for the Tidewater section of the state. Archaeologists have found it very helpful in their efforts to locate the village sites of the Indian tribes of that period.)

Speck, Frank G. *The Ethnic Position of the Southeastern Algonkin. American Anthropologist,* 26 (1924), 184-200.

—. *Chapters on the Ethnology of the Powhatan Tribes of Virginia.* Heye Foundation, *Indian Notes and Monographs,* 1 (1919), 223-455.

Stern, Theodore. *Chickahominy: The Changing Culture of a Virginia Indian Community.* Reprinted from the *Proceedings of the American Philosophical Society,* 96 (1952).

Stanard, Mary Newton. *The Story of Virginia's First Century.* Philadelphia, 1928.

Stewart, T. D. *The Finding of an Indian Ossuary on the York River in Virginia. Journal of the Washington Academy of Science,* 30 (1940), 356-364.

—. *Excavating the Indian Village of Patawomeke (Potomac), Explorations and Field Work of the Smithsonian Institution,* Washington, (1939-1940), 79-82.

Stith, William. *The History of the first Discovery and Settlement of Virginia,* Williamsburg, 1747. London, 1753.

Strachey, William. *The historie of travaile into Virginia Britannia, expressing the cosmographie and commodities of the country, together with the manners and customs of the people.* London, Hakluyt Society, 1849. Reprinted. Ed. by L. B. Wright and Virginia Freund. London, Hakluyt Society, 1953. (William Strachey came to Virginia in 1611 and served as Secretary of the Jamestown colony until 1613. He returned to England in that year and wrote his book perhaps within two or three years after his return. The vocabulary of the Virginia Indian language, of about 800 entries, which forms a part of the book, was no doubt prepared in Virginia. Strachey's account is very similar to that of Smith, but it is frequently much clearer and more complete.)

Swanton, John R. *The Indians of the Southeastern United States. Bureau of American Ethnology*, Bulletin 137 (1946). (This work is a collection of the richest source materials garnered by one of the great students of the American Indian.)

—. *The Indian Tribes of North America. Bureau of American Enthnology*, Bulletin 145 (1953). (This work gives the names, and locations of the Indian tribes of the various states of the United States, and the place of each tribe among the tribal groups of the continent, and some information relative to the role the important tribes played in the history of our country and in that of the States to the north and south of us.)

Swem, E. G. *Virginia Historical Index*. Roanoke, 1934-1936. 2 vols.

Tisdale, John W. *The Story of the Occaneechees*. Richmond, 1953.

Tyler, L. G. *Narratives of Early Virginia, 1606-1625*. New York, 1907.

Voegelin, Erminie. *Mortuary Customs of the Shawnee and other Eastern Tribes. Indiana Historical Society*, 2 (1944), 227-444.

Willoughby, Charles C. *The Virginia Indians of the Seventeenth Century. American Anthropologist*, 9 (1901), 57-86.

Wise, Jennings Cropper. *Ye Kingdome of Accawmacke, or, The Eastern Shore of Virginia in the Seventeenth Century*. Richmond, 1911.

APPENDIX

— Prehistory of Virginia —

The archaeologist has found it convenient and useful to think of the prehistory of the eastern part of the United States in terms of periods. These periods are not always characterized by totally different cultural features but they are sufficiently different to justify such a time tool. Radiocarbon dates have been obtained for some of these periods in several eastern states but much more work needs to be done before a reliable chronology can be expected. Therefore, no one can be too assertive about the time periods for eastern archaeology.

The prehistory of Virginia will be described briefly in terms of these periods and treated for the most part as state wide. The dates given here are suggestive for Virginia and are based largely on work done in other nearby states. The periods are as follows:

Period	Probable Time
Paleo-Indian	8000 B.C. –3500 B.C.
Archaic	3500 B.C. – 500 B.C.
Early Woodland	500 B.C. –A.D. 500
Middle Woodland	A.D. 500 –A.D. 1000
Late Woodland	A.D. 1000 –A.D. 1600
Historic	A.D. 1600 – present

Paleo-Indian Period. The first men in Virginia were nomadic hunters who roamed through the hills and valleys in small groups probably as early as 9,000 to 10,000 years ago. Their economy was based on the hunting of large as well as small animals, and the abundance or scarcity of game determined their movements.

The very fact that these Paleo-Indians were not numerous and were frequently on the move has made it difficult for the archaeologist to find a sufficient number of their artifacts at one location to determine the presence of a site. It was not until 1949 that the first camp site and "workshop" site of Paleo-Indians was discovered in Virginia (Dinwiddie County). This has proved to be a pure and extensive site and has added to our knowledge of the Paleo-Indians of the eastern United States.

These early hunters developed a very distinctive fluted point, with a concave base, and almost parallel sides which curve near the tip. Two hundred and sixty-nine points of this type have been found in the state and recorded. Typologically they are similar to the Clovis fluted points which have been found in the western part of the United States in association with the remains of the mammoth and mastodon estimated to be 10,000 to 12,000 years old.

The Paleo-Indians sought the finer stone materials for making their implements. Chert, jasper, and rock crystal were preferred to quartz and quartzite which were so popular with the later Indians. The assemblage of the stone artifacts they left behind consists of choppers, end scrapers of the snub-nosed variety; side scrapers, drills, gravers, fluted points, knives, blades, and cores.

About 3500 B.C. changing climate conditions, and the presence of recently arriving Indian groups produced changes in their way of living during the beginning of the Archaic period.

The Archaic Period. In this period the people preferred to live on hilltops or on slopes which were not too far from streams. They had learned to like shellfish, and their campsites are sometimes found near the source of this kind of food. But they wandered far and wide in search of other foods such as animals, fish, birds, and wild plants. Their sites are usually small but they are richer in artifacts than the Paleo-Indian sites because the people were more numerous, and because they revisited the sites from time to time.

Bows and arrows were not known in this period, but a throwing stick or spearthrower was used in throwing the spear in order to give it greater force. These throwing sticks had attached to them a ground stone object called bannerstone, which may have given balance to the implement, or which may have had a purely supernatural significance to the owner. The bannerstone had a hole drilled through the center to fit it on the throwing stick.

Several types of projectile points have superseded the distinctive, fluted point of the Paleo-Indian period. Some are straight stemmed with wide shoulders, others are stemmed and have narrow sloping shoulders. The stemmed points with bifurcated bases apparently belong to this period. A variety of scrapers occur, and hammerstones and flaked choppers are also present.

Near the latter part of this period, these people were making full grooved axes, soapstone bowls and crude pottery. The soapstone bowls or pots were usually rectangular in shape, with flat bottoms, and a lug or handle at each end. The clay from which the pottery was made was tempered with crushed steatite or soapstone and cord-roughened on the exterior. The shape copied that of the soapstone pots.

The Early Woodland Period. The rather simple culture during this period is based upon hunting and food-collecting. More attention was given to food-collecting, and the people were not quite as dependent upon hunting as they had been in the past. The small villages were scattered along the rivers and creeks, and the houses or shelters forming them were no doubt rather solidly built.

In a large part of the state three pottery series occur on many sites of this period. One is composed of a group of pottery wares made of clay containing crushed steatite for temper. The pot forms are oval and rectanguloid with flat bases. The second series is composed of a group of pottery wares made of clay with coarse temper particles of rounded river pebbles. The vessels are straight sided or nearly so, with rounded bottoms. The exterior of a high percent is net impressed and roughened. The third series, and the latest in this period, is composed of a group of pottery types made from clay mixed with fine quartz sand. Preference for cord-marking over the exterior is evident. The forms of the wares consist of open bowls, globular-bodied jars, and tall jars with straight sides. All have conoidal to subconoidal bases.

Stemmed points are somewhat more popular in this period than the notched. The blades are usually thick, and the flaking is coarse but very well executed. Full grooved axes and oval hammer stones are present.

Bannerstones were no doubt still used and stone gorgets were perhaps beginning to appear.

The Middle Woodland Period. Small village sites of this period were usually located along the streams and although the people were still primarily hunters and gatherers of wild food, there are evidences of some agriculture. The bow and the arrow were probably introduced in the latter part of this period, but it is very likely that the javelin and the spear-thrower continued to be used.

The burial mounds in the Piedmont and in the western part of Virginia form part of the middle Woodland Period. Burial goods are frequently found in these mounds and indicate that the people had real concern for their dead, and had developed an important funeral ritual.

Pottery shows some changes in the various ceramic areas of the state. There is a gradual decrease in the use of coarse sand and pebble temper, followed by an increase in fine to medium sand temper. Net impressed and fabric impressed are the most popular surface treatment. In the tidewater section pottery made from clay mixed with crushed shell makes its first appearance. In this area the pots have straight to slightly expanding sides with rounded and conical bottoms. Elsewhere in the state, the pot forms can be described as open bowls, globular-bodied, and rounded-bodied with rounded and conoidal bases.

A large variety of shapes of projectile points is characteristic of this period. Well made, delicately flaked corner-notched and side-notched points are most prevalent. A rather large triangular point is also present. Typical ornaments are ground slate gorgets, bone and shell beads, and antler combs of the central and north central part of the state. Grooved axes, especially the three-quarter grooved type, celts, tubular pipes of clay or stone, platform pipes of stone, usually soapstone, are also typical.

The Late Woodland Period. Most of the villages in this period were built on the low lands along the rivers and creeks in order to have available the rich soil for growing crops, and the food provided by streams. More emphasis was now placed on agriculture, Tobacco, corn, pumpkins, and beans were apparently cultivated. Hunting and fishing were still, however, very necessary to provide sufficient food. Many villages throughout the state were palisaded, and the houses were well built of poles set in the ground in a circular or rectangular fashion, bent and tied together at the top, and covered with bark or mats.

Investigation of ossuaries in the Tidewater section indicates that the bodies of the dead were placed on raised platforms until the flesh had fallen away, then at the appointed time the bones were gathered, wrapped in bundles, and were deposited, during a mass burial ceremony, in a large common grave or pit. Farther westward, the dead were buried in small pits, one or several burials to a pit, in or very near the village.

Pottery fragments are more plentiful than any other artifact of this period. Pottery is well made and shows some variations for each ceramic area. In the coastal area a high percentage of it is made from clay mixed with crushed shell. Fabric impressed is the preferred surface treatment. In the southeastern area practically all the pottery is made from clay using a fine medium sand for temper. Fabric impressed is very popular here also. In the central and north-central area the pottery is typified by a high percentage of crushed quartz temper with the clay. Fabric impressed surface treatment predominates here also. In the south-central area a medium to coarse sand is used for temper, and net and fabric roughened surface treatment predominates. There is a higher percentage of combing of the interior in the pottery of this area than in any other. In the Alleghany area, northern and southern, there is one series (Radford), which uses crushed lime for temper, and another series (New River), which uses crushed shell for temper. In the former knot roughened and net impressed are the most popular surface treatments. In the latter a high percentage of plain surface is present. In general the pot forms for this period vary. There are rounded, globular, and medium forms, with rounded or conoidal bases.

Small triangular points, celts, elbow pipes of stone and of pottery, decorated shell gorgets, an abundance of shell and bone beads, and implements of bone are additional important traits of this period.